Healed for His Glory

My Journey from Pain to Purpose

Karen Haag

DEDICATION

To my Lord and Savior, Jesus Christ. May You be glorified through this book.

> *"Glorify the Lord with me; let us exalt*
> *his name together."*
> Psalm 34:3

CONTENTS

ACKNOWLEDGMENTS

I gratefully give immense credit to my best friend and husband, Darryl. He supported me for many years when it seemed as if I'd never get my manuscript ready for publishing. Darryl's dedication and help to the very end have been priceless.

I also want to thank all my friends and family who helped make this memoir possible. I cannot begin to name those of you who assisted in this journey. You know who you are, and more importantly, God knows.

Thank you, Melanie A. Martin, for your belief in this book and for the editing you provided to clean up my work.

Appreciation also goes to Bill Wegener for the cover design.

INTRODUCTION

This book is about my journey with physical suffering. I have shared in detail about my pain, which is a big part of my life story. I'm convinced that the purpose of my suffering was to glorify God.

Jesus also experienced excruciating pain. Mine wasn't as bad in light of what Jesus endured, and, in no way do I claim that my suffering was anything similar to that of our Lord's. The good news is that the scriptures say He understands our pain. I'm a living testimony to that promise. Jesus not only understood my pain but, He chose to heal me from my pain in a miraculous way, which is why I wrote this book.

We all know that the Bible contains stories of people whom Jesus healed; there's more, however, to the stories than just physical healing. There's certainly more to my account than just my physical healing. My life had other plots and subplots, all purposely intertwined with my illness and healing.

Each time I hear *Not For A Moment*, a Christian song by Meredith Andrews, I get teary-eyed. The lyrics remind me of the darkest time in my life—a time when even though I'd wandered far from God, He was still there with me.

Through it all, He was working in my life. Even though His plan was quite difficult at times, it turned out to be a much better plan than I could have imagined.

God came to me at the time of my healing as a torrential downpour! Just as Hosea tells us, He's going to come. (Hosea 6:1-3) I feel as if I am one of the unfaithful Israelites. They always appeared to be straying from God. Many biblical characters are described as turning from God. We see this for the first time with Adam and Eve in the garden!

I can be counted among the ones who have met Jesus, know Him personally, and yet still need to be reminded to trust Him, to fear Him, to follow Him, and to glorify Him. Sadly, I miss the mark way too often. Even after having a most glorious experience with my Lord and Savior, I still fall.

Just because I've felt the very touch of God on my life doesn't mean that I'm a perfect example of a Christian. Just as the Israelites, I still flounder and fail. The good news is that we all serve the God of second chances!

My husband and I have a friend who wanted to visit me, approximately a year after she had learned that I was no longer living in pain. She had recently begun working with my husband again, who had once been her boss. She moved back to the area and worked in my husband's office for a few months, just long enough for us to get together and allow me to tell her my story. She was thrilled that my "higher power" revealed himself in my life in such a powerful way.

"Karen, you must tell your story," she urged. "It gives hope to others to know that their 'higher power' is at work in their lives." We soon realized that we disagree on *who* our higher power is. For me, it's God Almighty, Jehovah God, the Creator of the universe, the Alpha and Omega, the one true Savior of the world!

My prayer is that my story brings glory to this great God, the author and perfecter of my salvation. I pray that you can identify with my story and be encouraged. Maybe you will find hope as you read about, or be introduced to for the first time, our great God. He truly cares for His children. May we be reminded that our only hope is in Christ.

Our hope is the knowledge that those of us who have trusted Jesus will live forever with Him in Glory. Romans 15:13 reminds us: "May the God of hope fill you with all joy and peace as you trust in him, so that you may overflow with hope by the power of the Holy Spirit." Let's not forget Psalm 86:12, which reads, "I will praise you, Lord my God, with all my heart; I will glorify Your name forever."

May you be blessed as you read my story of struggle, healing, and surrender.

Karen Haag
North Wales, Pennsylvania

CHAPTER 1

THE BEGINNING OF MY FAITH JOURNEY

I was raised the fourth child and only girl in my family. My dad was a helicopter mechanic. Mom was a stay-at-home wife and mother.

It seemed Mom had two families to raise. When I was a toddler, I had two teenage brothers and a preschool brother. I can't imagine raising both teenagers and preschoolers at the same time. However, by the time I was 10, my older brothers were both out of the house—one in college; one in the U.S. Air Force.

I was a brat, plain and simple. A girl after three boys! Yes, there were privileges that I know I got at a younger age than my brothers, but that's probably partly because of my personality too. I am stubborn, and as the baby of the family. I always wanted, and typically got, my way.

My mom was the one who took us to church. When she and Dad married, she quickly found a church nearby to attend. At that time, a great aunt of mine attended the same church. My mom attended the church, Grace Chapel in Havertown, Pennsylvania, thirteen years or so before I was born. It was a great church, and I'm very thankful that Mom was fervent in consistent attendance. I don't recall if my older two brothers attended. By the time I was three, they were teens and had stopped going.

We didn't talk about Jesus at home that I remember, but Mom took us to church every Sunday morning. Dad, however, was the one who taught me the prayer, "Now I Lay Me Down to Sleep."

My dad would call my brother and me to his bedside so he could pray this prayer with us. Dad didn't attend church with us, but he felt it was his responsibility to teach us to pray before bedtime.

At Grace Chapel, I listened intently to the stories depicted on flannel boards of Daniel and the lion's den, Moses, Joseph and his many-colored coat, Jonah, The Exodus, The Red Sea, and the life and death of Jesus. Of course, I also loved the stories of the blind beggar; Zacchaeus; Mary, Martha, and Lazarus; and many more. I loved attending Sunday School.

I heard the Gospel in Sunday School from the time I was an infant. I learned I was a sinner, could not get into heaven on my own, and that I needed to ask Jesus to be my savior. I knew I was separated from God. I'd learned that if I accepted Jesus and his payment on the cross for my sin, I could be saved from the penalty of my sin and receive everlasting life.

One night, my older brother leaned over the edge of the top bunk and said, I just asked Jesus to be my Savior. I said, "I want to." We both prayed. Jesus said to allow the little children to come to him. Mine was indeed a "childlike" faith. I only knew what a child could know and understand. In spite of my limited knowledge, God drew me to Himself.

Mine was indeed a "childlike" faith. I only knew what a child could know and understand. In spite of my limited knowledge, God drew me to Himself.

I don't know why He called me as a little child, but He did. I had a sense of peace after accepting Jesus as my Savior. I was only five, but knew I'd been saved. I also know that even though I sinned during those early years, I had a sense of right and wrong. I sensed the Holy Spirit's leading at times even when I didn't understand. I sometimes experienced "shaking" in my spirit when I knew the Lord wanted me to do or not do something. It doesn't mean that I haven't sinned or suffered; but my faith has always been a big part of me.

I was confident since I'd already asked Him to be my Savior that I would one day go to be with Him in heaven. But I didn't know anything about repentance and letting Him be the Lord of my life. As I grew older, I learned that there's a penalty for sin and that penalty is death. Death is eternal separation from God. Romans 3:23 states this clearly: "For all have sinned and fall short of the glory of God." Then we read in Romans 6:23: "For the wages of sin is death, but the gift of God is eternal life in Christ Jesus our Lord."

Sinners cannot enter heaven because God is holy and cannot permit sin in His presence. In Old Testament times, spotless lambs were slain for the sins of the people. God sent Jesus, His Son, to be crucified on a cross to pay the penalty of sin for all who believe in Him. Jesus, therefore, took the place of the spotless, or sinless, lamb to pay the price of sin once and for all.

The sovereignty of God allowed Jesus—the sinless Son of God—to be killed. Jesus was buried in a tomb with a massive stone rolled in front of it. This was to prevent robbers from stealing His body. However, on the third day, an angel rolled back the stone to reveal that Jesus was gone! Jesus had defeated death and had risen from the grave, just as God's Word had predicted.

I believe the Bible is the inerrant Word of God, written by men, at God's direction. 2 Timothy 3:16 states, "All Scripture is God-breathed and is useful for teaching, rebuking, correcting and training in righteousness."

"I believe the Bible is inerrant, written by men, at God's direction."

More than 350 prophecies recorded in the Old Testament have come true in Jesus. Hundreds saw Jesus after He rose from the grave. His followers died horrible deaths because they believed in Him. They knew Jesus personally and had witnessed His resurrection. These disciples were willing to go to their graves because they knew the story of Jesus was true.

When I was 14, I went to a haunted house operated by a Christian group. The Gospel was clearly presented to those who attended. My eyes were opened to the sacrifice Jesus paid for me. I committed my life to Him, got involved in the church youth group, read scripture consistently, and learned what living for Jesus meant.

I finally understood that when I accepted Jesus' sacrifice on the cross in payment for my sins, I was given the Holy Spirit as a seal on my soul. He would be my helper to comfort, teach, and guide me.

I met my husband, Darryl, at church when we were kids. We began dating as high school sweethearts, although we only had a few dates before we broke up. We then resumed our relationship while I was still in high school and he was in college. It was a rocky on-and-off-relationship, possibly because we were both the youngest children in our families. We decided not to stay together. We broke up in the fall of 1977. That didn't last. We were engaged by the next February and married in September 1978.

Our first child, Eric, was born in 1980. Graham was born in 1982, and Ashley came along two years later. We built a house in 1986 and began to raise our lovely family. It was idyllic. I believed I was spoiled; many things in my life always went my way. I had the perfect husband, family, and life. Yet I soon began to believe that I was not good enough. My thoughts about myself were far from positive. This negative belief system caused many problems in my family as well as deep down inside of me.

As I've matured in my walk with the Lord, I now realize that these thoughts were fiery darts from the evil one, Satan. Ephesians 6:16 tells us: "… take up the shield of faith, with which you can extinguish all the flaming arrows of the evil one." These thoughts are contrary to what I know to be God's truth. I try to cling to truth rather than listen to the lies of the enemy, Satan.

Before and during my trial of pain and suffering, Satan employed his lies to try and push me "off path" and he often succeeded. I'd get so caught up in his lies that I couldn't live a victorious, joyful Christian life. I've learned that I can't live for Christ in my own strength. I must trust in His strength in all things.

I've learned the hard way that I can't live for Christ in my own strength. I must trust in His strength in all things.

However, hindsight is 20/20. I realize that I've not always walked as close to the Lord as I should. As I ponder the years I endured the pain of RSD, I realize there were dark times in my spiritual life as well. I've learned that those are the times I'd allowed sin to pile up, unconfessed. Subsequently, I'd quenched the Holy Spirit's desire for me and was unable to sense His direction. I'm learning, after 50 years of being a Jesus follower, that Satan is a strong adversary, one whom I always must stand against.

When our thoughts are contrary to God's Word, we leave a door open for the enemy. We "hear" things that are untrue, such as that we are not good enough or can't measure up. These are Satan's tools that keep us from living victoriously. However, if we confess our sins as we are aware of them and walk closely to the Lord, we can more easily resist the enemy's attacks.

I'm a sinner saved by God's grace. This salvation only comes from the death of Jesus on the cross, where He willingly took on my sin. Because I am a believer in Jesus, everything in my life is influenced by His grace and what He did for me.

CHAPTER 2

CAUGHT OFF GUARD:
THE ONSET OF PAIN

I suffered severely with bronchitis in January and February 1994. The pain of my cough was quite intense. I was on three consecutive rounds of steroids, antibiotics, and asthma drugs to attempt to control the cough.

During that time, I was still helping at my kids' school and enjoying youth ministry at church several days a week. However, I was feeling overwhelmed by feeling so sick most of the time. Just trying to get myself ready and out the door each day was stressful.

Because of the medications I took each day, I was very hyper at times, yet, at the same time, quite lethargic. I couldn't sleep. I had no energy. So, I played Nintendo. I was engrossed in a competition with my son Eric as we played Donkey Kong.

I allowed Eric 45 minutes each afternoon to play. Then, the next day, I spent all day while he was at school trying to catch up to the point in the game that he'd achieved the day before. I don't think I caught up too often, but I must have kept up enough to see it as competition. (When I looked back on this time after my diagnosis, I realized that the repetitive motion of playing video games every day might have contributed to my pain.)

Life seemed quite hectic that year. I remember a prayer that I uttered one day during early spring. I prayed, "Oh, Lord. Get me off this merry-go-round that seems to be my life." I felt as if I were running from one thing to another. In hindsight, I never dreamed I'd fly off that merry-go-round and fall flat on my back.

I felt as if I were running from one thing to another. In hindsight, I never dreamed I'd fly off that merry-go-round and fall flat on my back.

Early in March, I went to the mall. It was my first outing after my extended illness. I strolled into a card store to purchase an anniversary card for my parents. Their 50th wedding anniversary was coming up; my siblings and I had a large party planned.

I walked out of the store carrying the thin bag and card in my hand. That was the first moment I realized that something was wrong. It hurt way too much to hold the lightweight bag in my hand. After switching the bag to my other hand, I found I couldn't hold it in that hand either. So, I stuck the bag under my arm. I thought, "That's weird." I figured I must have been experiencing some sort of arthritis.

I don't remember how much of the issue of being unable to grasp bothered me as I was preparing for my parents' party. However, I began to notice when I was busy or working much that my hands were swollen and painful the next day or even two days later.

I was the one doing most of the party planning. I was hosting the party, even though my sisters-in-law also contributed. I was cleaning the house and was determined to complete a wall stenciling project in the kitchen before everyone arrived for the big celebration. I remember the pain that I experienced as I stenciled, yet it wasn't debilitating.

The week of the party arrived. It was a very stressful week. I was planning a significant event for all the family to enjoy, and everything went wrong. My husband was out of town, so that intensified all the things that seemed to be going amiss.

The laundry had piled up, and there was much cleaning to do since we had family members whom we'd invited to stay with us. I can't remember all that happened, but the clothes washer died, and then the basement flooded on the day my brother's family was arriving from New Mexico.

By Friday night, all the family had arrived. I was suffering from excruciating pain. I didn't tell my mom because I didn't want to upset her. I believed she would have felt guilty if she'd known I suffered from pain as a result of hosting a party for her.

My brothers and their families lived far away, so when they visited Philadelphia, the first thing they wanted to eat was hoagies. When I was in high school, Mom had a job making hoagies. She was known for making delicious ones. We needed twenty hoagies when the entire family gathered at my house the night before the party. It was typical for us to make them ourselves and much cheaper than purchasing them from a restaurant or store.

I stood next to mom to help make the hoagies. One of my sisters-in-law could read my face and see that I was in pain. She offered to help without mom catching on as to why I needed help. That night, I rested and recouped a bit with sleep. I had pain the following day, but it did not slow me down very much.

The anniversary party was a great success! Many family members came to celebrate my mom and dad who were a favorite couple in the extended family. The event was a memory that I cherish.

We had a great time together Saturday at the party, but then my niece, Kerry, from New Mexico, was rushed from the party to the hospital. She was a sweet girl who suffered from spina bifida, yet she never let it stop her from doing what she wanted. She spent a couple of weeks in the hospital in Philadelphia, about 90 minutes from my house.

While my niece was hospitalized, I realized my pain was getting worse. And it was beginning to keep me from being at the hospital with Kerry as much as I wanted to be. Her mom, Marcy, suggested I may have carpal tunnel syndrome and should try wearing braces at night. So, I wore braces the next couple weeks, but the pain and discomfort didn't improve.

I was a hairdresser before Darryl and I married. I enjoyed my profession. After our first baby was born, I retired, yet continued to work occasionally. By the time the pain started, I was volunteering once a month, at the county jail for female offenders, cutting hair. I was also giving haircuts and perms at home.

We had a grown foster daughter, Dawn, at the time. I gave her a perm on a Friday afternoon. (She was living on her own;

yet we still were involved in each other's lives.) Then, Saturday, the pain in my hands and wrists was so bad that I couldn't give our 9-year-old, Ashley, a perm. I felt awful since I had promised. I told Ashley that once my hands got better, I'd perm her hair. (By the time I was healed years later, perms were out of style and she still hasn't gotten that promised perm!)

I was in a great amount of pain after that last perm. I also realized that I was having difficulty performing my roles as a wife and a mom. That was the last straw. The advent of the pain meant I couldn't do hair any longer. I had to give up working at the prison.

If I couldn't do hair, which I loved, without it affecting me taking care of my family, I had to do something. I didn't want to give up my stylist role, but I knew it was necessary. Little did I know that I'd be forced to give up hairdressing, but I'd also be surrendering many more of the activities I enjoyed.

Sometimes God asks us to surrender what we love to do. I do not doubt that I was meant to be a hairdresser. I certainly enjoyed the profession I'd chosen. And I do not doubt that God had other plans for me—plans other than me just growing old as a hairdresser. As of this time in my life, I still enjoy cutting Darryl's hair and occasionally that of others, but I have no desire to work as a professional in a salon.

I believe God changes the minds of His children. I see now that God was preparing to use me to glorify Him. He changed my direction from that of a busy mom, hairdresser, and youth leader to someone who would later pen a manuscript filled with hope! Sitting down to write was certainly never on my mind until God changed my path. Not only did He change my path, but He also brought a new purpose to my life.

I believe God changes the minds of His children.
I see now that God was preparing to use me to
Glorify Him. He changed my path . . .

I also believed God was preparing to free up my schedule. This would mean that I'd have more time later to devote to my mom. I'd be free to give my mom her final desire—the desire to live her last days with me. I know enough about myself to know that if I'd not gone through the pain and suffering, and, more importantly, my total surrender to God, that I would not have been as loving, patient, and kind to my mom as I was able to be. I was not the perfect caregiver by any means, but I know I treated Mom better than I would have had she been in my care before my healing and surrender.

God certainly changed the path of my life in 1994. These verses, once a bit tough to read and not quite as "personal," now bring me peace and joy. I know I can trust Him in all aspects of my life. This verse, for sure, is a fabulous promise: "For I know the plans I have for you," declares the LORD, "plans to prosper you and not to harm you, plans to give you hope and a future." (Jeremiah 29:11)

Let's not forget the wisdom of these words: "You make known to me the path of life; you will fill me with joy in your presence, with eternal pleasures at your right hand." (Psalm 16:11)

My prayer is that as you continue to read this book, you will understand that God loves you more than you will ever know. He wants to lead, direct, and possibly change your path to bring glory to Himself.

CHAPTER 3

A FRIGHTENING DIAGNOSIS

The summer of 1994, I was diagnosed with Reflex Sympathetic Dystrophy Syndrome (simply referred to as RSD) or, as it is now called Chronic Regional Pain Syndrome (CRPS).

RSD is a progressive disease of the autonomic nervous system, and more specifically, the sympathetic nervous system. It is the overfiring of nerves that sends pain signals to the brain long after an injury has healed. For example, if the patient recently has had surgery, stubbed a toe, suffered a heart attack, or had an infection, which is what happened to me, instead of recovering, his or her pain level *increases.*

The disease typically affects one or more of the patient's four limbs, but it can occur in any part of the body and can spread to other areas. A good description of RSD can be found on the web site, www.rsds.org.

Some symptoms of RSD are chronic, burning pain, inflammation, mottled skin, emotional issues, and sleep disruption. Extremely sensitive skin and excessive sweating are also symptoms. The pain level of RSD is ranked as the most painful form of chronic pain by the McGill Pain Index, a measurement tool that medical professionals use to determine their patients' degree of pain.

Patients may experience many other symptoms throughout their affliction with RSD. Not all patients exhibit all symptoms, which may change over time due to the stage the patient is in, medications the patient is taking, treatments, and factors such as time of day, month, or season. Also included as a consideration is whether the patient is enduring extreme stress.

I hadn't thought that my pain was severe enough to see a doctor until I knew I could no longer do hair and take care of my family. I scheduled a visit with my family doctor. She ordered physical therapy for a diagnosis of carpal tunnel syndrome. Several physical therapy locations were located near me; however, I chose one a bit farther from home. I soon realized that God guided me to this location. He led me to a therapist who was a Christian. She was a great encouragement to me during my treatment. Together, we were able to trust the Lord and talk of His goodness as she treated me.

All the therapists there were very gentle, kind, sweet, and helpful. I first went for six weeks of physical therapy and had no progress. I believe I was getting worse. My therapist said I needed a different diagnosis for the center to best help me. According to law, she couldn't tell me what she suspected, nor could she treat me with her diagnosis. But, because she understood RSD and had been trained in treating it, she was suspicious and believed it was indeed what I suffered.

I was encouraged to give up everything I didn't have to do. The belief was that if I could give up being active, then I could eventually manage my pain. So, I surrendered even more pieces of my ever-busy lifestyle.

If I could give up being active, then I could eventually manage my pain. So, I surrendered even more pieces of my ever-busy lifestyle.

I was a busy mom of three. I crafted, sewed, stenciled, knitted, and crocheted. I was busy helping at our daughter's school and served as a youth group sponsor at church. I gave it all up. Soon, it wasn't long that I *couldn't do* any of those things. I couldn't prepare meals without help, and my days as the family chauffeur were limited.

At my therapist's urging, I returned to my family doctor. She ordered an EMG (electromyography, a test of the nerves of the muscles), which was a very painful experience. Ashley volunteered to go with me that day. I used to take my children with me when I needed injections. If one of my children was with me, I seemed to endure the pain of needles better.

Ashley didn't enjoy that day's experience any more than I did. At almost age 10, she could tell I was in a lot more pain after the treatment than I had before we'd left home.

My family doctor then sent me to an orthopedic doctor armed with a list of my symptoms. This doctor wasn't sure what was going on with me. The orthopedic doctor suggested I see a rheumatologist, so I made yet another appointment.

A dear friend, Carol, attended our church. She had struggled with pain and other terrible symptoms for a few years. At times she suffered from intense pain levels, which rendered her unable to care for herself. Carol's pain began when a ream of paper slid off a shelf and hit her arm. She went to more than 50 doctors before she was finally diagnosed with RSD and began receiving treatment.

Before my pain started, I had visited Carol during one of her especially difficult periods. She was in a hospital bed in her living room and required almost total care. I prayed for her after that visit, asking God to take her to be with Him in heaven. I didn't understand what she had, but I knew she was in terrible pain. I hated seeing her suffer so much. However, she eventually received treatment that allowed her to improve and get out of bed. I was grateful that God knew better than I did in allowing her to live through that awful season.

One day that summer, Carol called me. She said our pastor's wife had told her about my health issues. Our pastor's wife, a nurse, believed that maybe Carol and I suffered from the same illness.

My sweet friend so very tenderly asked me what was going on. She listened for a while and then said, "Karen, I'm afraid to say it, but I think it's possible that you have RSD. You need to see a rheumatologist." It just so happened that she had called the morning of my first appointment with a rheumatologist— *her* rheumatologist! Of course, I didn't believe that this was just a coincidence.

Carol was quite relieved to know that I had an appointment with him because he knew about RSD, would be able to diagnose it, and could send me to the correct doctor for treatment. Can you imagine the horror I had when I learned that I might be suffering from the same illness as my friend, who had, at times, been utterly bedridden with pain?

At this step, Carol's doctor was the third doctor I would see. Another dear friend, Julie, wanted to go with me. It was typical for her to step in when I needed help; however, in retrospect, I know the hand of God was in her offer. I certainly needed her support as I left the office that day.

After talking with me and examining me, the doctor left the treatment room for a few moments (I believe, to refresh his knowledge of RSD). He knew enough of RSD to be suspicious that indeed I suffered from it, but the illness wasn't one of his specialties.

The doctor returned to the exam room. I could see that he had something serious on his mind, and it didn't appear to be good. He asked if I had ever heard of RSD. I could tell he wasn't thrilled with having to inform me of this syndrome. It is not a diagnosis that a doctor wants to give a patient.

I answered that I'd heard of RSD and that I knew his patient, Carol. The relief and regret on his face were evident when I told him that I knew Carol.

He was relieved that he didn't have to explain to me what it was, but he regretted that I was suffering from the same symptoms which were destroying my friend's life. When he had left the exam room, he could only find one online article that described RSD. He printed it and handed it to me as I left his office.

In the mid-1990s, there wasn't much information available to patients. However, we had a ListServe, an email service that sent messages between members (popular in the early days of the Internet)—this service connected RSD patients. Then, in the early days of personal web sites, I developed a web site, RSDawareness, where I attempted to explain this horrible syndrome and connect people to other helpful websites. A section of the site was dedicated to self-help ideas that I had gleaned from the ListServe. (My site is no longer available; however, many people found me and appreciated having someone to talk with who also suffered from RSD.)

Writing this book has helped me to remember some people with whom I became friends during those early days. I enjoyed the RSD online presence, supported others, and received support myself. Darryl and I even attended a few seminars conducted by the man who ran the RSD ListServ. I also wrote and printed a brochure to help others understand RSD. The brochure helped both patients and family members better understand this ugly disease. Even my mom was eager to distribute copies of the brochure.

After a few years, I realized that I needed a break from the Internet. It was time to live life with my illness. I knew I should no longer spend so much time dwelling on the disease and the awfulness of it. It was the right decision for my family and me to back off of social media interactions. We chose to be involved with more positive things in our lives.

The rheumatologist made an appointment for me with a specialist he wanted me to see. However, the appointment was six weeks away. When we were faced with the possibility that I had RSD, I was devastated. I remember fear, anxiety, and panic because wasn't resting in God's sovereignty at that point.

I was devastated. I remember fear, anxiety, and
panic because I wasn't resting in God's sovereignty
at that point.

I spoke with Carol again, and she stressed to me the need to get treatment as quickly as possible. The possibility for a successful remission is highest in the first three to six months, and slightly possible for up to a year after the injury that caused the pain. At this point, I was already at month five.

Darryl was unable to go to the rheumatologist with me, yet he was quite involved in my diagnosis and concerns. I shared with Darryl that the doctor had diagnosed RSD, the same illness that our friend had. Darryl took me in his arms and said, "If this was what the Lord has for us, we will deal with it." And we did.

It wasn't always easy and sometimes it was more than I felt I could handle. But I had hope that this next doctor would be my hero, correctly diagnose me, and start me on an appropriate treatment. I'm glad I didn't know what was coming next. I wish I had trusted the Lord more and doctors less. I would have saved myself from panic, fear, and devastation.

Today, I find myself encouraged by God's promises such as this passage from Isaiah 41:10: "So do not fear, for I am with you; do not be dismayed, for I am your God. I will strengthen you and help you; I will uphold you with my righteous right hand."

This passage also reminds us not to fear: "Be strong and courageous. Do not be afraid or terrified because of them, for the LORD your God goes with you; he will never leave you nor forsake you." (Deuteronomy 31.6)

During my time of suffering, I allowed fear to overtake me. The fear was like a paralysis, preventing me from looking to the Lord as I should have. I was not always aware of the fact that He was in control of my situation. But God was always faithful. He was *always* there even when I didn't notice His presence.

> *I allowed fear to overtake me. The fear was like a*
> *paralysis, preventing me from looking to the Lord*
> *as I should have.*

I probably wouldn't have made it through the suffering in those trying years if I hadn't had the Lord with me. If I'd truly rested in His Sovereignty, I wouldn't have reacted as poorly to the information I would soon receive from the next doctor. However, I realized that God was leading me to the place where I could find rest and refuge in Him

CHAPTER 4

MY SEARCH FOR TREATMENT

A t this point, I assumed I had a diagnosis, so the search now began for appropriate treatment. I was about to be sorely disappointed. Even though the rheumatologist had diagnosed RSD, each subsequent doctor I saw pronounced me as "undiagnosed."

It wasn't until after I saw the rheumatologist that I compared my list of symptoms to a list of RSD symptoms. They mirrored my symptoms exactly. However, I didn't have one symptom on the list that I'd shared with the doctors—night sweats.

I compared my list of symptoms to a list of RSD symptoms. They mirrored my symptoms exactly.

My night sweats were so bad that I'd wake up sometimes to change my nightgown. After I saw that list, I realized that I needed to tell the doctors about the sweating. I hadn't yet told them because I hadn't connected the night sweats with my aching wrists. However, just by adding night sweats to my symptoms list, it made much more sense to the doctors.

Another struggle I faced in trying to achieve a proper diagnosis was that I didn't believe I'd suffered from something traumatic that had brought about my pain. Because I didn't know that infections could bring on pain such as mine, we didn't make the connection between the bronchitis I'd had and the subsequent onset of my pain.

The third doctor, the rheumatologist, sent me to his friend, an orthopedic doctor at a prestigious Philadelphia hospital. My rheumatologist had called while I was in the office and talked to his friend who agreed to see me. I waited six weeks to get in, and all the while the pain was progressing. I was eager for the weeks to pass quickly because I fully expected to get help from the orthopedic doctor.

During the time I waited to see the orthopedic doctor, we attempted to move on with our typical summer activities. We had a pool in our backyard which we all enjoyed immensely. I was pleased that we had an activity for our family to enjoy while I was confined to home, suffering from pain. It took quite a bit of convincing to get the kids to help with the pool. Typically, I was the one who vacuumed, cleaned, and monitored the chemicals. Now it was their turn to pitch in with the pool maintenance.

At last it was time for my long-awaited appointment. I just knew this doctor could help me. Because of his friend's referral, he had kindly scheduled an appointment for me that was 45 minutes before his usual opening time. When we arrived, Darryl and I were quickly escorted into an exam room to wait, knowing I was the doctor's first patient of the day.

Due to an emergency, the doctor arrived 90 minutes late. The waiting room had filled with patients. We could see the doctor checking my chart outside the exam room. After a brief moment, the doctor charged into the exam room. He immediately reached to grab my hand, and I quickly pulled it back from him. It was undoubtedly an instinctive gesture because I could barely dress at that time due to the pain.

I knew I didn't want that doctor or anyone else for that matter, shaking my hand. He scolded me and murmured something to the effect that he was disgusted with me and all the "other RSDers" for protecting our affected limbs from additional pain.

Without talking to us about the reason for the visit, what was going on with my health, or providing an exam, he said, "You don't have RSD. It's in your head." With that ugly, verbal blow, I believed I was back at square one. I have no idea why I didn't consider returning to the previous doctor, except that he'd strongly suggested I needed someone else besides himself to treat me.

Darryl and I were both stunned, and I was intensely angry. I was freaking out. I can only imagine how I sounded to my parents. We had driven straight to their house after that appointment since they lived between our home and the doctor's office.

I was also quite scared because we had already waited six weeks to see this specialist. Now, I was past the six-month mark for a possibility of the disease being in remission.

When a patient was suspected of having RSD back in the mid-90s, the first thing medical professionals recommended was a nerve block. This was the best diagnostic tool available at that time.

In the procedure, called a stellate ganglion block, the doctor injects a local anesthetic into the nerve area in the neck, on one side of the voice box or the other depending on which arm was involved. These procedures are usually performed in a series of three blocks within two weeks.

The theory was that a block of the sympathetic nerves works somewhat like a computer reboot—you first shut down the system, and when you turn it back on, hopefully, it is "fixed." If this block in any way gave relief from the pain, then the likely diagnosis was RSD. However, the desired result was a complete "shut down" of the pain, effectively putting the RSD into remission. Just as in a computer reboot, "the computer," or the nerves, in the case of these blocks, do not always "come back" repaired. At the time of my treatment, these types of blocks were the best option for achieving a possible remission.

I used to share with other RSD patients that they needed to consider their diagnosis just as urgent of a diagnosis like cancer. My diagnosis certainly felt urgent to me. If a doctor tells you that you have cancer and need surgery as soon as possible, you schedule the surgery. And with RSD, if a doctor says he needs to perform a series of nerve blocks, you must take quick action.

I learned from many people online that their doctors wanted to perform nerve blocks, but these patients believed that such a first step was too drastic. However, as with cancer, time is of the essence. For me, I knew that if I genuinely were suffering from RSD, a series of nerve blocks was not only diagnostic, but this treatment was the best chance for my illness to go into remission.

Because this most recent doctor on my list of doctors said I didn't have RSD, I knew it would be even longer until I could get the nerve block treatment that I believed I needed. I was not happy at all at yet another delay.

I was not trusting in God's timing for these treatments that I so desperately needed. I thought it was in my power or should be, to obtain these treatments. I was convinced by this time that I suffered from RSD and that I *must have* a series of nerve blocks to get relief or put my illness into remission.

I was frustrated, sad, and angry at the delay. And I was not praying. I had tried to take control of my situation. Maybe I was under the delusion that I could be in control and make things happen as I wished.

While I was still at my parents' house and in a panicked state, I called the fifth doctor, a neurologist. He was also located in Philadelphia. I do not recall precisely how I'd heard about him, but I was glad I called him. Maybe he would be the missing link to my story?

I wish I could say that in my panic we stopped and prayed that the Lord would lead us to the next thing we needed to do. But we didn't. I failed at the point in calling on the name of the Lord. God showed His faithfulness despite my unfaithfulness. I have no doubt that God brought to my mind the name of the doctor in Philadelphia whom I needed to call that day.

I failed at the point in calling on the name of the Lord. God showed His faithfulness despite my unfaithfulness.

I arranged for an appointment for that Friday. When I arrived at the office, the waiting room was empty. The doctor didn't have regular office hours on Friday afternoons, but he kept his Friday afternoons open for callers who were frantic for help. If there weren't any such calls, he would have the afternoon off. In my emotional panic, I guess I sounded like someone who needed to be seen as soon as possible.

I was grateful that he had this policy for desperate patients such as me. I felt I was blessed to have been given this time of his. I believed that he had this scheduling plan so that he could accommodate people like myself who were suspected of RSD or any other time-sensitive issues.

The neurologist spent a few hours with me in his office as his staff conducted tests on me. He truly listened to what I had to say and what had been happening. He believed I suffered from RSD; however, the test results seemed inconclusive. The neurologist decided to send me to a pain center connected to his hospital. He also wanted me to see a vascular specialist, the sixth doctor I'd see, to determine if anything else was occurring that could be contributing to my suffering.

That fall of 1994, I continued my quest for treatment. It was not until two months or so later before I received treatment. I spent this time mostly on the sofa with my hands covered in a blanket, watching television. I watched many cooking shows; however, I certainly couldn't stand in the kitchen and make any of the dishes. At times, I'd grab a post-it-note and jot down the recipes. I have many of these recipes in my recipe box, still untried.

The vascular specialist ordered an MRI and a doppler ultrasound to study the blood flow in my arms and legs. The result of the ultrasound was a diagnosis of Thoracic Outlet Syndrome (TOS), a part of my problem. (We never knew if the TOS were a result of the RSD, or if it were in addition to it.)

I also had the MRI, which was an incredibly traumatic experience. By this time, my shoulders were as painful as my wrists had been. The intense pain meant that I was unable to raise my arms without significant pain. The MRI technicians asked me to lie on the bed of the machine and stretch my arms up over my head. They presented a small, half-circle tube of plastic in which I was to place my hands with the inside of my wrists touching to keep them in position. The pain was incredible. I tried my best to hold this position during the screening, which seemed to take an eternity.

I spent more than an hour in the MRI machine as the vibrations and sounds rang in my ears, both sounds making my pain worse. Then, the technicians pulled me from the machine and asked that I bring down one arm by my side so they could put an IV in to look for contrast. This resulted in even more pain. The technician who attempted to put the IV in had no luck, so they went to get the radiologist.

All the while, I still had one arm up and one arm down. I remember crying and wishing that just one of the people in the room would place a hand on my leg and comfort me. I felt very alone and isolated—a prisoner in my pain.

Somehow I had to get that arm back up over my head and positioned next to the other one, without moving the rest of my body or the second arm. I wished I could call out for my mommy, who was in the waiting room.

During those many days of physical suffering, seeing doctors, undergoing tests and treatments, I was fearful of many things. In His Word, God tells us 365 times "do not fear." Did you catch that? Three-hundred-sixty-five times—a reminder for *each day of the year*!

However, I was still quite fearful. I was afraid of the pain and fearful that I would not receive the care I needed in a timely manner. I was also dreading the thought of being an invalid for the rest of my life, like my friend Carol. I was afraid of not being the wife and mom I desired to be.

I was still quite fearful. I was fearful of the pain and fearful that I would not receive the care I needed in a timely manner.

Instead of leaning into the Lord and seeking refuge in Him, I eventually sank into a deep and stifling depression.

CHAPTER 5

THE BEGINNING OF MY TREATMENT

In November 1994, I was sent to see two doctors—a pain management psychiatrist and an anesthesiologist. These doctors were located at the pain center connected to the same well-known Philadelphia hospital as the neurologist and the vascular doctor I had already seen. Together, these four, and possibly more doctors, practiced a multidisciplinary approach to treatment.

Doctors from a variety of disciplines met in a "roundtable" setting to discuss each patient they treated jointly. I saw this approach to patient healthcare as brilliant. I knew the combined expertise of these professionals would be more than valuable to my treatment plan.

I knew the combined expertise of these
professionals would be more than valuable
to my treatment plan.

Depression is a significant symptom of RSDS. However, sometimes a stigma exists regarding Christians and depression, or the need to see a psychiatrist for emotional or mental concerns. I've known many Christians who frown on the idea that a Christian would have problems that warrant visits to a psychiatrist.

When I called to make an appointment at the pain clinic, I was scheduled two appointments—one with the anesthesiologist, and the other with a pain management psychiatrist, whom I was informed every patient must see. So, I accepted the appointment with the psychiatrist, so that I could ensure getting in also to see the anesthesiologist. My first appointment was with the psychiatrist. He diagnosed me as depressed (in addition to my physical pain) and prescribed an anti-depressant. I wasn't pleased with this solution, but at this point, I was willing to try anything that may help.

I learned that anti-depressants are also used for pain relief and shared with many people that I was taking an anti-depressant because it could help keep me from getting depressed, and it could help manage my pain. I honestly believe that it did help relieve some of my pain.

For many years, I denied that I was depressed; however, as I look back, I was. The fact, too, that RSD physically causes depression, coupled with constant pain, certainly could cause anyone to fall into depression. And of course, I was depressed.

Many RSD patients are afraid to seek psychiatric help because almost every RSD patient has at one time or another been told: "it's all in your head." Of course, we knew that such a comment was untrue. We were ashamed to think that anyone—doctors, family, or friends—would believe that it was just a psychological condition, but many of them do. We were also afraid that if people around us knew we were seeing a psychiatrist, it would be "proof" that our pain was not physical.

It is quite essential to the RSD patient's well-being to see a psychiatrist. The patients have many strikes against them that lead to depression. The input and expertise that a psychiatrist provides are invaluable.

Dealing with pain around the clock is as good a reason as any to have a professional practitioner to talk with regularly. After a couple of years, I only saw the psychiatrist annually. He was my favorite doctor and the one whom I saw consistently throughout my long ordeal. He was the one I trusted the most to help me make changes in my treatment plan and medications. This doctor also tracked how I managed my depression.

Later that same day, I saw the anesthesiologist. A resident was trailing him and both of them listened intently to what I had to say. They discussed the possibility that I may have myofascial pain syndrome and fibromyalgia.

Myofascial pain syndrome is a chronic muscular pain disorder. Fibromyalgia and RSD have many shared symptoms since both occur because of the over-firing of nerves. Fibromyalgia is the over-firing of the muscle nerves, and RSD is the overfiring of the sympathetic nervous system. However, after careful thought and discussion, the doctors discounted the fact that I had either of these illnesses.

The anesthesiologist was intent on helping people with their pain. He said that even if he didn't know my *exact* diagnosis, he could help me with the pain. I believe he suspected RSD because the treatments he suggested were ones typically used to diagnose and treat RSD.

No single test definitively diagnoses RSD; the medical community uses various medications and modalities that help control the pain that accompanies this horrible syndrome. If what they do helps, the illness possibly could be RSD; however, diagnosis of this illness is never black and white. It's no wonder so many patients visit multiple doctors for diagnosis and treatment.

The first medication the anesthesiologist prescribed was Clonidine, a blood pressure medicine, being used experimentally at the time for RSD patients. I left that visit quite encouraged. I believed I was finally getting help.

When I went back two weeks later, the office staff asked if I'd noticed any change. I responded that almost immediately I realized that my skin sensitivity had lessened. That was what they'd hoped the Clonidine would do for me if indeed I had RSD. The relief continued gradually. At least I now felt as if I were headed in the right direction.

The relief continued gradually. At least I now felt as if I were headed in the right direction.

One of the first treatments I had, besides the Clonidine and the anti-depressant, was the nerve blocks in my neck. Finally I was getting the long-awaited blocks, which I'd been hoping to get for six months.

Because I had pain in my hands, wrists, and arms, I was scheduled in December 1994 for two series of three nerve blocks. I would receive one round on each side of my neck during a three-week period, for a total of six. The hope was that this treatment would put me into remission, and if not remission, provide a firm diagnosis of RSD.

Yet again, I was facing even more painful needles. To knowingly subject myself to more needles was a true testament to the pain I suffered. But I had no idea what was coming with the first block. The fact that I returned numerous times is the proof I needed for myself that I was indeed in such pain and that it wasn't in my head as some believed. The irony of this needle treatment was that it was used to determine if the patient had a syndrome that could result from a trauma as simple as a needle prick. Yet here I was, now subjected to many needles in the hope of an accurate diagnosis and proper treatment.

I still considered this treatment to be "torture" that I was willing to experience. The technicians asked that I stretch out on my back on a gurney. They put a hard "pillow" under my neck and stretched my head back until the top of my head touched the bed. This was a weird position to maintain as well as being quite uncomfortable. Shouldn't doctors themselves be forced to experience the very treatments they put their patients through? Maybe if this were the case, doctors would become a bit more understanding!

Out of the corner of my eye, I saw the syringe, which was unlike any other needle I'd ever seen. It looked to be at least eight inches long and relatively large in diameter. Then I spied the tube of a mixture of lidocaine and another one or two anesthetics, which was at least an inch in diameter, if not larger, and about six inches long.

I laid physically still yet freaking out mentally. The pain of being stuck with a needle in the front of my neck and knowing the team would be plunging the needle near my spinal cord was horrible. Receiving that first treatment was a painful experience that left me physically shaken and emotionally traumatized. To top it all off, this first block was performed without a sedative.

I later called Carol and told her about my experience. She told me that the patient could request a sedative, but that doctors don't like to offer it because it meant a doctor must be present to insert an IV. Wow! *What?* Patients must endure great physical pain when they have a *choice* to request a sedative? I was stunned, to say the least.

Carol further explained that being sedated would mean a longer time in recovery than if the patient were to undergo the procedure without a sedative. She added that the medical team would prefer that the patient receive the block without a sedative because there was no recovery time needed after the procedure.

Beginning with my second block, I requested a sedative! My recovery time was longer than most, but I suffered much less from the procedure than I had from that first horrendous experience.

I'd started watching the new television show, ER, that fall and I loved it. The show took place in a teaching hospital where medical students performed treatments they had never before seen performed. I was going to a teaching hospital for treatment and had no problem with students "practicing" on me. But imagine my fear when I overheard a new student being introduced around the room. I then heard the staff take her into the room next to where I was lying to await my procedure.

I heard someone ask the student if she knew what a stellate ganglion block was. When she said no, they used a diagram on the wall to explain it to her. I was lying there thinking, "They aren't going to let her do it on me, are they?" I don't know why I didn't ask, but I didn't. I don't know that I would have challenged them at that moment anyway.

This particular student was indeed the one standing over me when I was wheeled to the procedure room. I think she was as nervous as I was. When she finally plunged the needle into my neck, the pain was beyond anything I'd ever experienced.

An electric shock went shooting through my body. She had hit a nerve. "I'm so sorry," she said apologetically. My doctor was not pleasant, as he snapped at her for apologizing to me. I was dumbfounded to hear him because I genuinely appreciated her sincerity. The doctor coaxed her to continue the procedure, then in frustration he took the needle from her and continued the procedure himself. That was certainly a time when I was more than grateful for the sedative I'd received.

Another time, my in-laws took me to get the block treatment. Theoretically, these blocks were used for the upper body. But that day, somehow, maybe as a result of the sedative, my legs were wobbly and unsteady. Afterward, I couldn't use my arm on the side that had the injection. That wasn't a normal reaction, but the technicians must have been successful with getting the anesthetic mixture in the right spot.

After my treatment, we headed back to my van. Because my arm and legs were not cooperating, I could not climb into my vehicle on my own. My mother-in-law pushed me from behind up into the van. I look back now and laugh about it, but I didn't think it was amusing at the time. We were on a busy street in Philadelphia where many people watched as an older woman pushed me on my backside to get me into the van!

The blocks were tortuous, yet I returned numerous times because I knew they helped me. I don't believe the procedures ever completely eradicated my pain. Still, they did reduce the pain level to the point where the Clonidine and the anti-depressant seemed to be more effective than they were before the blocks.

I most likely was suffering from RSD, but we were not exactly sure. Yet my treatments were based on the genuine possibility that it was RSD. In the shape I was in, I didn't care what it was that I suffered from as long as my pain was manageable. I knew that the blocks and the Clonidine were RSD-specific treatments and that these two were indeed helping me.

We celebrated Christmas that year, although with me out of commission, it wasn't quite as perfect as I usually preferred. I was one of those people who were overly concerned with the "the stuff" that had to get accomplished by Christmas, such as decorating and crafting gifts for the school and Sunday School teachers. This was my first year of being unable to go to my usual extremes for the holiday. But it was also the first year that we learned we didn't need all of the trappings to celebrate Christmas.

This was my first year of not being able to go to my usual extremes for the holiday. But it was also the first year that we learned we didn't need all of the trappings to celebrate Christmas.

I remember the special gift we bought the kids that year—a computer! Everyone seemed to be purchasing computers, so we did too. I remember as Darryl and I drove home from the store, he asked for what I saw myself using the computer. I replied that I didn't believe I'd be using it much at all because of how my hands hurt all the time. And I wasn't even sure for what I would use the computer.

Darryl spent half of the night Christmas Eve installing the software. Little did I know that I would have to learn how to use the computer. Our computer was more advanced than both the one Darryl used at work and the ones our children used at school.

I didn't know how to use a computer, but I set out to at least gain a general understanding so I could help my kids and husband. I turned out to be the family's technology expert. At a time when everything else was just too painful for me to do, time on the computer gave me an outlet—something productive to do—as long as I limited my time typing.

Combined with the relief in the severity of my pain that both the blocks and Clonidine gave me, I believed that the anti-depressant was starting to make a change in my outlook.

We went into that new year of 1995 feeling hopeful. Hopeful that I was getting medical treatment that was helping. Optimistic that the physical therapy I would resume would help and that I'd continue to increase my activity level. And I was especially hopeful that God indeed was with me through this season. This was something I would have to be reminded of again and again.

CHAPTER 6

THE PATH OF PRESCRIBED MEDICATIONS

I finally felt as if I were on my way to feeling better. At least I was getting the help I needed.

The treatment of RSD is different for every patient. No specific medication or treatment modality is used primarily for RSD. Doctors who treat RSD patients use a variety of medications and procedures such as physical therapy, nerve blocks, acupuncture, heat therapies, and aqua therapy.

Finding a doctor who is well versed in the treatment of RSD is not easy. Patients must be willing to try new medications or treatments and not give up just because one particular thing didn't work for them. I was blessed to locate doctors relatively quickly, even though at the time I thought I'd never get the help I so desperately needed. Because Carol was coaching me, I knew I had to be patient and work with the doctors until we could determine the best solution for me.

I now know that God was in control of my situation all along, even though I didn't *feel* Him there. He was faithfully with me; I just didn't allow myself to rest in His guidance.

I now know that God was in control of my
situation all along, even though I didn't feel Him
there. He was faithfully with me; I just didn't allow
myself to rest in His guidance.

The combination of medications that I took was a "fine-tuned cocktail," which changed at times over my years of treatment. Through trial and error, after many years, we finally determined what worked best for me. We also learned that I could only add or stop medications once in six months.

I reacted well to most medications, almost too well at times. I began a new prescription at an exceptionally low dosage, well below the FDA recommended dosage. Over time, we slowly added more until we found the best dosage that I could handle and that gave me the desired result. It took a long time for me to increase the dosage up to the recommended amount. Even though I took powerful medications at times, my dosages were conservative, always at the lower ends of the approved amounts.

Besides the original anti-depressant and the Clonidine, I took many different anti-depressants, anti-seizure drugs, opioids, and sleep aids throughout my illness. Clonidine was experimental when it was first prescribed for me, and it worked well. However, as a blood pressure regulator, the medication caused my blood pressure to lower.

Even as I was taking low dosages, the effects of Clonidine made me groggy, dizzy, and tired because my blood pressure dropped. I couldn't function. The Clonidine was the only medication that I took the entire course of my illness. Because it helped me so much overall, the doctors continued to raise the dosage so that I could gain more and more relief from my pain. The more I took, the less I was confined to the sofa with my hands covered, resting them on a pillow.

After a few years, I had adjusted well to the Clonidine and became more active, even though I was still a bit groggy. With almost every new doctor I encountered over the years, he or she would try to lower the dosage, but my sensitivity level would always increase. I took Clonidine for almost 18 years.

Many people would say, and many RSD patients will agree, that there was no way they would put up with the side effects of this medication. Yet, I was willing to continue to live my life as usual as possible with the grogginess. Overall, I appreciated the pain relief I received from Clonidine.

RSD causes insomnia, so helping an RSD patient get the rest and sleep she needs is especially crucial to pain management and healing. I suffered from insomnia and mostly slept during the day while my husband and kids were at work and school.

I tried sleeping pills to help me sleep during the night. I experienced hallucinations and hives with the first two prescriptions. We eventually found one that seemed to help. I soon stopped taking any sleep aids, believing that they didn't help enough to justify the horrible side effects. During the time that Ashley was in college, I was taking a sleep aid that caused me to fall asleep at awkward times, such as when taking communion at church, sitting on the toilet, or sitting at red lights.

I was taking a sleeping pill regularly when I flew to Indiana to visit Ashley at her college, Taylor University. One day, in our rental car, we were driving, headed back to Ashley's dorm after an outing. I remember asking Ashley if I had just changed lanes because I did not remember doing so. "Yes. Why?" she asked. "I must've fallen asleep!" I exclaimed. We were quite nervous until we arrived back at her dorm. Unfortunately, I couldn't let her drive the rental car, but I knew I wasn't a safe driver at that point.

Ashley was more like a "mothering sister" than a daughter at times. She grew up rather quickly. I'd been ill since she was nine. We were a team taking care of each other. I leaned on her to help me a lot, maybe too much. Those trips to visit her at college were hard on me physically, but I needed to see her. I had relied on her at home for so many years that I struggled with letting her go away for college.

I was also working at this time since the kids were gone, and we had two in college. I found a job I could do as an answering service operator, which I enjoyed for more than a year. But, I had trouble getting up in the mornings and getting to work on time. I finally quit both the job and the particular sleeping pill I was taking because I realized that I just couldn't continue with either. I was fearful of being fired from my job because of tardiness and grogginess, and I thought the side effects of the sleeping pill were just too risky and dangerous.

Over the years, I had become as stable as possible for a person with RSD. I'd become somewhat of a success story for doctors because I didn't frequently need more and more pain medications. I'd learned that I could do more on my own to relieve a pain flare-up. These flare-ups occurred when the pain became more severe than my usual, daily chronic pain. The flare-ups were sometimes frequent, such as when I'd done too much, the wind was blowing hard, or when the barometric pressure changed.

The good news was that I didn't need to go to the doctor often for help. I often chose to endure the increased levels of pain by soaking in my tub, which I loved. I began to see success, which resulted in me being dismissed from one of my doctors.

Even though I was doing well, I didn't require higher dosages of my medications, nor did I require expensive treatments. Overall I wasn't showing any month-to-month improvement for the doctor's practice to justify keeping me as a patient. (To me, this dismissal was similar to dismissing a person with diabetes because his insulin was working well and maintaining a correct blood sugar level; the patient still had diabetes.) Being dismissed by a doctor who was helping me was quite frustrating because doctors who know how to treat RSD patients are few and far between. However, in their defense, they had few, if any, patients who suffered from the same illness that I had. Their business was to provide treatments, which at the time, I no longer required. I just happened to be an exception. It was just not typical for an RSD patient to be so stable on medication alone. So, at this stage, the doctors didn't know how to deal with me.

At the time, my anger at what I thought was their injustice to dismiss me blinded me to their side of the story. My passion was driven by my fear—fear of needing to find another doctor immediately so that my medications would not be interrupted.

My anger was driven by my fear—fear of needing to find another doctor immediately so that my medications would not be interrupted.

I'd been told that once you get the RSD pain under control with medications and then get off those prescriptions, the pain could return worse than before. It was also possible that the pain would be quite tricky to get under control again. I was always extremely fearful of losing my pain medicines. I certainly didn't want the pain to worsen.

By this time, the kids were out of the house. I was alone a lot and started allowing my fears to overcome me. I was not trusting in God but trusting in myself to make sure I got the pain relief I needed. I liked believing I was in control. Several years later, I realized I was *not* in control and I needed to place my trust in the One who was.

I liked believing I was in control. Several years later, I realized I was not in control and I needed to place my trust in the One who was.

I found yet another anesthesiologist who specialized in pain. He decided I should try Fentanyl patches, which gave me great pain relief. The downside was that I lost sleep. The pain relief from the patches was great, but the loss of sleep was of grave concern to my doctor. So, we discussed a new medication—Kadian, a once-a-day pill that's a slow release form of morphine.

Kadian gave me constant pain relief. This was something new for me in the many years I'd been taking opioids. Now, I had 24 hours of pain relief. I remained on the lowest dosage of Kadian a few years.

In 2007, Darryl received a wonderful job offer and we moved from North Wales to Pittsburgh soon after I began taking Kadian. Our boys were on their own. Ashley had just graduated from college and had also moved away.

By this time, I was in a dark place emotionally. I needed something new and exciting. We were both ready for a change. I'd never lived anywhere but in the greater Philadelphia area. I was eager to move, but the move meant I had to find a new doctor to prescribe my "medicinal cocktail."

The first doctor I went to was in a well-known Pittsburgh hospital pain clinic. That doctor did not work out, and in my panic to find another doctor, I contacted the head of the clinic. I requested that they contact my pain management doctor in Philadelphia to verify my diagnosis. I was quickly referred to another doctor in that same clinic.

My new doctor was fantastic! The first time I saw him, he gave me an article to read—one that was co-authored by my favorite doctor, the excellent pain management psychiatrist whom I appreciated so much. Now, in my new city, I had hope that I was again on the right track.

During the time of our move, I also found myself in the process of trying to find a new anti-depressant. I needed one that would help stabilize me with my dislike of being around people. I could not handle commotion, and I suffered from motion sickness. Of course, I still had pain and depression. Surely I wasn't asking too much of one, simple medication?

Soon after our move, significant breakthroughs occurred in the treatment of fibromyalgia. Two new medications were released specifically for the nerve pain associated with that syndrome. Because of the similarities between RSD and fibromyalgia, my doctor thought I should try these new meds. I tried Cymbalta, which was an anti-depressant/pain medication. This proved to be extremely helpful for me. I was now much more able to cope with commotion, noise, and crowds.

My life and our family's life were much improved with this new suite of medications—Clonidine, Kadian, and Cymbalta. And just to think—it only took 15 years to get the combination precisely right! I am so thankful for those medications because I believe they helped me arrive at my turning point, which began in 2010. I became more outgoing and more willing to be with people. I also started getting more involved at church. And, of course, this new change led to my revival, which I will share later.

The intensity of my pain those fifteen years was horrendous. But it was more than just nerve pain and depression. I also suffered from a great many other symptoms.

I must share just how horrendous this illness was and how it affected my family. The extremes of pain versus the glories of healing are utterly amazing. Only God can get credit for what happened next.

CHAPTER 7

CHANGE OF LIFESTYLE

For most of the 18 years I suffered from RSD, my symptoms included pain, swelling, extremely sensitive skin, insomnia, excessive sweating, weakness, and depression. These were the most significant symptoms I had; however, as I mentioned earlier, there are many symptoms of RSD.

Sometimes the pain was aching. Sometimes, I felt as if my wrist, arm, or leg were broken. Other times, the pain shot through a limb. Cold sensitivity was also an issue. When I got cold, my bones felt as if I'd been outside in the harsh and extreme winter temperature.

The feeling was as if I'd been outside for hours shoveling snow, building a snowman, or sledding, and my wrist or wrists had been exposed to the elements. It's a bone-chilling pain that I even experienced on a 90-degree, sunny day if I didn't have at least one extra layer of clothing on my wrists.

So, I had a perfect solution. I wore cut-off sock tops on my wrists. How cute I looked as I shopped in the grocery store in the middle of the summer, wearing a short-sleeved shirt and sock tops on my wrists! Even children stopped to ask why I was wearing socks on my wrists. I responded graciously, explaining the "why," rather than appearing upset that they'd asked. If I were wearing a long-sleeved shirt or even a sweater over the shirt, I still required the sock tops. I'm not sure why, but I always needed an extra layer for warmth. I was the sock-tops lady for a long seventeen years.

I had first tried tennis wristbands made of stretch terry cloth, an idea I got from my son, Graham. When he was six years old, he had a fascination with tennis wristbands. No matter how hot it was outside, he wore them. He wore them constantly for a year or more before we learned the actual reason. We just assumed Graham was being his wonderful, quirky self. I used to say he always walked to the "beat of a different drummer." We loved that aspect of his personality.

One day we learned that Graham was sporting the wristbands to cover a mole on his wrist. Before he began covering his wrists, someone in his class at church had pointed out his mole. This made Graham feel uncomfortable. I, on the other hand, had never given that little mole any thought. Graham was determined to cover the mole. At first, he wore long-sleeved shirts all the time, even in the summer. Then he found wristbands were a neater solution and they became his constant companion.

I wouldn't have considered removing the mole just because it bothered Graham; but his reaction was strong to something so small. After speaking with Graham's pediatrician, who was concerned that the mole could be cancerous, we decided that a dermatologist should examine the mole. After this doctor examined his mole, we chose to have it removed.

The doctor said that one parent needed to stay with Graham for the procedure, so without hesitation, Darryl said, "I can tell you it won't be my wife!" I was (and still am) a bit squeamish.

Our little boy was so excited to get the mole removed that he didn't need any help holding still. He watched the entire procedure and promptly told me afterward that the surface under the mole looked "like pizza under the cheese." Graham being Graham, he asked for pizza for dinner—of course! We obliged.

Graham sported wristbands to cover his mole; I wore them to keep my pain level down. In the end, we both wore them for the comfort they gave us. I'm not sure I would have ever thought of wearing something on my wrists if Graham hadn't worn wristbands many years before. But tennis wristbands proved to be too snug for me; hence, my need for sock tops, which seemed to work best. I just wish I could've had my issue removed in one quick procedure as efficiently as Graham's was removed.

Graham sported wristbands to cover his mole; I wore them to keep my pain level down. In the end, we both wore them for the comfort they gave us.

My hair was not exempt from the torture of RSD. Occasionally, I noticed that my hair had grown extremely fast. One year, I noticed the opposite—I lost quite a bit of hair from the top of my head. This hair has never grown back. Many RSD patients also lose their arm and leg hair. I lost most of the hair on my arms the years that I had RSD.

My nails also grew fast or got brittle and broke. These visible symptoms were always a blow to my already low self-esteem. I continued to get more down on myself as more symptoms occurred, yet there wasn't much I could do about these symptoms. So, instead, I began to try not to care about how I looked or what I wore. The bottom line was that my comfort was most important.

My internal thermostat was also on the fritz. If I were cold, I couldn't make myself warm. When our children were home, and I lay on the sofa with my hands on a pillow, shivering, they'd pile on afghans until I finally had warmed up. Then they removed a blanket at a time until I felt that I wouldn't overheat or get cold with too few.

If I got overheated, I'd drink ice water to cool off, and often I'd end up drenched in sweat from head to toe. This was yet another embarrassing condition and a blow to my self-esteem, especially when I'd be in public and suddenly my hair was soaked and my clothes were sticking to me.

Another RSD symptom was swelling. At times, I was swollen to the point that my clothes barely fit. Then the swelling would go down and everything would fit again. The swelling usually came after I had done too much activity with my arms or my legs. In the beginning, I didn't see my knuckles for more than a year. I'll never forget my physical therapist exclaiming, "Look! We can finally see Karen's knuckles."

I couldn't stand to cross my legs or have one leg on top of the other in bed. It felt as if my bones were grating on each other. I couldn't even tolerate my husband's limbs resting on mine. I hurt from the touch and dripped sweat at the point of impact. This same sweating occurred once when I was holding a baby and our skin was touching.

Early on, when the pain was at its worst, I had trouble touching things. My hands were extremely sensitive to anything with texture or hard edges. Silverware hurt my hands, so I used padded arthritis flatware. Once I forgot to take my Clonidine, the drug that helped with my hypersensitive skin. We had hamburgers for dinner and the bun was too rough and painful to hold. I was also quite sensitive to the fabric of my husband's shirts. He enjoyed wearing a particular blue one to bed and it hurt my hands immensely just to touch it.

We had been a reasonably touchy family, giving each other lots of hugs and kisses. Then suddenly, I couldn't handle being touched. One day Ashley sidled up as close as she could to me without touching me and I flinched. I didn't want her to notice, but she did. She was so hurt. "I didn't touch you, Mom." "I know," I said, "but your shirt sleeve touched mine and that was enough to cause me pain." How awful.

As I improved from the medications, this type of instance decreased. We were never as physically affectionate as a family after the RSD struck us; that is, until my healing. I just realized that's probably when I found out that Graham gave great big bear hugs for which he became well known.

We were never as physically affectionate as a family after the RSD struck us; that is, until my healing.

Physical therapy is a usual way of life for many RSD patients. My first experience with PT was at the therapy office in Kutztown I had chosen. Kutztown was not far from our house in Breinigsville. The therapists there treated me so well and seemed to care about me. I especially enjoyed the modalities they used to help me.

One such modality was an outdated and rarely used fluidotherapy machine stored in a back room. The machine contained ground-up corn cobs that blew around in hot air. I sat with my arms in the machine. The goal was to desensitize and warm up my constantly freezing hands and wrists. I endured therapy that first year mostly because I enjoyed that machine.

Hot wax therapy was also a successful treatment for me. After I'd completed my exercises at the therapy center, the technicians dipped my hands in a plastic container of water. They measured the swelling in my hands by seeing how high the water level was when my hands were in it. Then, they'd dip my hands in the hot wax several times, wrap them in a towel, and let me rest. They would then remeasure my hands in the water to see if the swelling had decreased.

I benefitted greatly from gentle stretching massages on my neck and arms. After the massage, my therapist attached a TENS unit (Transcutaneous Electrical Nerve Stimulation), which blocked the pain signals to my brain through electrodes on my skin. I'd then be wrapped up in hot pads for 15 minutes to relax and allow the benefit of the TENS treatment to work. This treatment worked so well for me that I was prescribed a portable TENS unit for use at home. I used this unit every day; it was a constant on my wrists for many years.

After a few years, I was prescribed aqua therapy, which was the most soothing form of physical therapy exercise because it was easier on my joints. After I learned the exercises, I wish I could have gone to any indoor pool each time we moved, but the water in most heated indoor pools was set at approximately 84 degrees. At that temperature, I froze. And of course, being cold and shivering led to more pain. So, I couldn't just join any club with a pool; I had to locate a physical therapy site that had a pool in which the water was more than 94 degrees.

Hot tubs were quite helpful when we traveled. We'd always try to locate a hotel with a hot tub. I could do several of my therapy exercises in the hot tub. I wasn't always in therapy, but I ended up back in physical therapy a few times over the years.

My family called me a compulsive "weeder" in those days. If I returned home from an outing, or if I were wearing my Sunday clothes, a weed would catch my eye and I felt compelled to pull it. You can't imagine how much self-control it took when I saw a single, out-of-place weed in someone else's yard! I loved weeding because both the action of weeding and the warm sun was therapeutic.

One beautiful, warm afternoon I was weeding and reached under the edge of a bush by our walk. I must have disturbed a hive of ground wasps. I was stung at least a half a dozen times. I'd been stung before, and I'd not only felt the pain of the sting, but I'd also feel a shock wave of pain spread throughout my body. The result of a single sting could put me in bed for three days, weak and exhausted.

But this time, having been stung by so many angry wasps at once, certainly had long-term consequences. The pain it caused was just too much for my body. Instead of three days in bed, I was there for three weeks. Then, I returned to physical therapy for six months after I recovered from the attack.

For many years afterward, I had persistent pain in my neck and couldn't sit without propping my head up with my hand. I've since suffered from whiplash, and, although the pain was intense, I could still hold my head up on its own.

When I think back to those days after the wasp attack, I am overwhelmed by the pain, depression, and the feeling of helplessness I experienced. This was indeed a time that I needed to see the pain doctor for help rather than just trying to get through the pain by myself. I felt as if I'd returned to square one. With time, aqua therapy, and patience, I again got back up and began to live more happily.

Ironically, I have no clue why wasps and bees were so attracted to me before and during my illness. I got stung several times while I had RSD, but since my healing, I've not been stung once.

Other pain-inducing things occurred in my life that I couldn't avoid. My saga continued, but in new and interesting ways.

CHAPTER 8

PAIN, MY CONSTANT COMPANION

Vibrations of any kind caused me more pain, sometimes while the vibration occurred or even a day or two later. Music, especially organ music or concerts, resulted in great pain. I think it was the vibration from the bass notes. Even though sitting through a concert was difficult, it wasn't until later that I'd feel the full effect of the vibration that I'd experienced. That's how it was with most things that caused the pain to get worse. I'd pay later in pain and weakness and end up on bed rest.

Planes and automobiles were a huge source of my suffering; the combination of noise, commotion, and the sun caused pain. Plane flights, especially, were excruciating for me. We tried to book window seats for me and middle seats for Darryl. If we couldn't get these, then I took an aisle seat and Darryl sat next to me to buffer me from the other passenger.

The aisle seat posed a different problem with people bumping me as they went past. I would lean way into Darryl so I could prevent being touched by someone in the aisle. The drink cart was just as much of an annoyance.

We traveled by plane at times but knew it would cause me pain or that I'd spend a day or two recovering afterward. Frequently, I'd require up to two or three weeks of recovery after a trip, so we planned our trips carefully. I carried a pillow onto the plane to put under my feet because the vibration was intense and more than I could tolerate. Yet, now when I fly, I don't even notice the vibration under my feet.

We drove to Michigan to visit family in August 1994. This was my inaugural trip with RSD—where I first learned how very much pain I'd suffer from traveling. When we finally arrived after a 15-hour car trip with three children, I was in pretty bad shape. My whole body was "buzzing," which was a term I used to describe the feeling I had as if I were in an electrified body of water.

Travel of any kind caused the pain to flare. I didn't have a firm diagnosis at this point and I didn't appear to be any different, so it was difficult for my other family members to realize how hard life was for us.

I may have looked the same or "normal" on the outside, but when we were in our room, Darryl dressed me because it was just too hard for me to do myself. My pain level, especially the sensitivity of my hands and fingers after the trip, was very high. I couldn't touch my clothes, buttons, or zippers.

My extended family was confused with my condition, mostly because they'd not heard of RSD. My sister-in-law shared later that she remembered seeing me for the first time, sitting on the balcony, wrapped up in blankets, and looking miserable as if I'd given up. She later apologized for something she said during that summer vacation. I don't remember what she said, and I think because she later became my greatest supporter during those years, I didn't dwell on it.

My sister-in-law . . . remembered seeing me for the first time, sitting on the balcony, wrapped up in blankets, and looking miserable, as if I'd given up.

She attempted to help me out of the depressed state she believed I was experiencing. I needed my family to understand that I didn't want to be in pain or unable to participate, but I was suffering and needed to recover from the long drive to Michigan.

My children didn't know how to handle my situation, so how could others outside of our immediate family? At times, I appeared fine, and then I'd crash and not be able to do anything for a while. I lived on adrenaline during those difficult years. It was as if a powerful medication was in my system. I wasn't able to accomplish much of anything unless the adrenaline "rush" had overcome me. Then, I was like a whirlwind and tried to accomplish whatever I could before I crashed.

At the point of the crash, I was totally depleted. It took another rush of adrenaline to get me moving again. The act of getting a family of five prepared for a vacation can drain any mom and result in her needing rest. When we were at home after a rush, it was easy to rest. But after that rush of getting ready for that trip, I had to travel immediately, which caused even more havoc on my body.

We took another trip a few years later, after I'd received treatment and was taking medications. This trip was to Cape Cod to celebrate my in-laws' 50th anniversary with extended family. We drove through New York City over the George Washington Bridge. It was rush hour and we got stuck in a traffic jam of tremendous proportion. We crept along over the bridge.

We had traveled at least two hours at this point. All the preparations of getting ready to leave home and the vibrations of travel had already increased my sensitivity to everything. I was getting more and more nauseous from the overstimulation of light, music, vibrations (including the bouncing of the bridge), and traffic sounds. I huddled in the back seat in misery. I was certainly not in any mood to be conversational. It was all I could do just to be in the vehicle and not in bed. Darryl and Ashley were in the front seats, enjoying their conversation and music.

I finally spoke up to say that I was miserable and needed help to minimize the onslaught of torture to my body. I hated asking them to change their routine. I felt like a selfish brat who just wanted her own way. I covered myself with a blanket and closed my eyes.

They turned off the music and spoke as little as possible. We finally arrived at Cape Cod. I can't remember what happened when we got there, but I think I must have gotten another rush of adrenaline because I felt "on" for my in-laws' anniversary. It was a grand weekend celebration with all the family together. Thankfully, we had a cottage to ourselves and I could withdraw and revive a bit between activities.

My family and friends frequently didn't understand what I was enduring. Unless an affected limb is red and swollen, others may believe that the patient is overly dramatic. However, parts of my body were quite tender, sensitive and full of pain.

*My family and friends frequently didn't understand
what I was enduring. Unless an affected limb is red
and swollen, others may believe that the patient
is overly dramatic.*

The fact that no one understood what I was going through
was exceedingly difficult. I'd either withdraw from people or try
to explain how awful it was. Some people seemed to understand;
others thought I was either exaggerating or making it all up.

Attending church was always uncomfortable. I eventually
learned to carry a pillow for resting my arms because the pain
was intolerable when my hands and arms were resting in my lap.
One church we went to had wooden pews. I had to purchase a
chair pad and take it along so I could sit comfortably.

In the summer of 1997, I suffered an intensely painful ear
infection. I remember being so scared during that time, believing
that the RSD symptoms would travel into my ears and face, or
other places. I didn't know if I could handle living with full-time
pain in those areas.

The pain in my ear subsided. However, my ankles soon
started to ache. The aching was the same as the pain I had in
my wrists initially when the pain began in 1994.

At my next appointment with my pain management psychiatrist and the anesthesiologist, I shared about the ear infection. Both doctors concluded that, yes, the RSD had spread to
my legs. I now had what they considered "full-body" RSD.

*Both doctors concluded that, yes, the RSD had
spread to my legs. I now had what they considered
"full-body" RSD.*

After the RSD jumped to my legs, I sometimes used a cane when my hands could hold one. When we went to the mall or somewhere with our family, I used a wheelchair. Then the grocery stores were so kind as to start offering those electric riding carts. I still struggled to reach forward and use the handles to steer. But I was grateful to get to go shopping with my husband and daughter.

About a year into my pain, Ashley had an assignment in school to design something that would help someone. She created an ingenious and beneficial "pillow" for the grocery cart. I used it to rest my arms on as I pushed the cart.

Even walking caused pain when my arms swung back and forth. I also couldn't touch the cart with my hands to push it. But with the design of my pillow, I not only had a place to rest my arms, but I could also push the cart. I used this wonderful invention many times until I was also affected in my legs. I'm sad that I finally disposed of that precious gift. I do, however, have the memory of Ashley's ingeniousness.

Even though I was able to go shopping, we had to keep the trips short until the stores began using mobilized grocery carts. I loved the freedom those carts gave me. Even though at times my hands and shoulders hurt from maneuvering the cart, I was glad to get back into grocery shopping. I still couldn't go on my own, but at least I was there and able to tell Darryl or Ashley what we needed to pick up. It was an awfully long process to shop with me in those days.

Not only was I unable to pick items up in the grocery store, but it also took me so long to travel the aisles. I had some form of motion sickness, similar to seasickness when I shopped. I couldn't move my head or eyes the way anyone would while shopping. I had to look at one section of the shelves on one side of the aisle and then look at the other side.

It was not always easy to distinguish what was on those shelves and what I needed or wanted. Most people have regular items that they purchase. They decide that a particular brand is what they want and they purchase it regularly. When they get to that item on the aisle, there's no need for a decision. They just grab the item and go. I, however, began to agonize over which item was the best buy for my money. It's taken me many years to be able to get to the "grab and go" stage again.

I also had trouble being in a conversation with more than one person at once. I felt seasick or motion sickness from conversing with a group. Moving my neck back and forth caused pain. Chatting with a group of people is something that has taken a long time to relearn.

Sightseeing also caused a type of sea sickness. We went to Ireland twice while I had RSD. The first opportunity came in 2003; and I was not going to allow the RSD to hold me back. I'd had it for nine years and had learned to live with it. I had always wanted to visit Ireland where my grandmother was born and many of Dad's relatives lived.

We flew into Manchester, England, where my dad's cousin picked us up at the airport. A day or two later, we drove over to a ferry port in Scotland. I was so excited when that ferry from Scotland docked in Ireland.

As we drove up the coast, I didn't want to miss a single sight, and there were new ones around every bend in the road.

My neck got stiff from looking around so much. I also became dizzy and tired.

But I couldn't stop looking and rest. I had to see the sights. I was very overtired as we drove through one small town. There, I saw a sign that caused me to burst out laughing. I laughed until I had tears running down my face.

My very reserved English cousin was in the car with me. I'm not sure she'd ever seen anyone laugh until they cried, especially over a sign. A sign that was probably common to her, but one I'd never seen before. It was an "elderly crossing" sign, depicting a small, bent-over man and a little old woman with a cane. These signs are located near retirement and nursing homes. It's a sign with significant meaning, but seeing it hit my exhausted and significantly depleted funny bone.

I tried wearing progressive lenses in my glasses while I had RSD, and I got a seasick sensation while wearing them. I later changed to bifocals to reduce the feeling of nausea. Conversing and sightseeing have both improved, but I still must remind myself that I can move faster and can look at both sides of the grocery aisle.

I rarely drove because it hurt my wrists, neck, shoulders, and arms. The motion sickness when I looked around was still an issue. I always planned to stop at multiple places while I was out. We scheduled my trips carefully, especially if I needed to go "to the other side of town."

After a few years with RSD, we sold my beloved minivan. I realized that I just didn't have the strength to drive the van but that I could better handle a smaller sedan. With the purchase of that new car, I now had more freedom to get around.

As time went by, I was slipping into a dark place. I was becoming more and more isolated during the daytime as well as during the long nights when I suffered from insomnia. I began listening to the swirl of negative thoughts in my mind. I continued to act and appear healthy on the outside. I still loved God. However, I was in a mentally dangerous place.

I began listening to the swirl of negative thoughts in my mind . . . I still loved God. However, I was in a mentally dangerous place..

My thoughts and the words that I was speaking to myself were not of God. They didn't reflect the truth that I knew from scripture. It was a long time before I was able to see the truth. It was a continuing journey of more pain and suffering.

CHAPTER 9

LIFESTYLE ADJUSTMENTS

W e quickly learned that my illness would result in many adjustments to our family's lifestyle. In particular, because of my intensely sensitive skin, we grew to be quite flexible.

In the early years of my illness, Ashley shampooed my hair because it hurt too much for me to lift my arms. Even if I could get them up, my hands hurt if I just touched my hair.

I felt as if my little girl grew up really fast and way too soon. Instead of me telling her if she needed a sweater or jacket, she told me if I needed one or not. And she'd taste my food and tell me if it were too spicy for me because my taste buds were overstimulated and extremely sensitive. Once I ordered my favorite Taco Bell item and assumed that the person who had prepared it had added hot sauce. But Ashley tasted it first said it was not too spicy.

I couldn't stand to feel air streaming from an air conditioning vent as it hit my skin. We had overhead fans installed in a house we moved into in 1996. Darryl and I couldn't use the fan in our bedroom. The pressure and movement of the air hurt too much. Clothing that touched my skin hurt me. A fly landing on my skin hurt me. Even a sleeve brushing up against my arm was painful.

The first year, I laid on the sofa with my hands on a pillow because everything I did caused pain. Air moving across my hands caused pain. I needed to keep the air from causing pain but every blanket or sheet I used irritated them. My mom took me to a thrift shop. We walked to the baby items section, where I found the oldest, softest baby blanket to cover my hands on that pillow. And found relief, sweet relief.

After the RSD traveled to my feet, I tried propping up blankets around my feet because of the pain if the covers touched my feet.

On rare occasions, I experienced another symptom that resulted in the scariest moments of my life. This symptom occurred when I overdid my activity, which resulted in too much adrenaline pumping for too long. After over-exerting myself, I'd lie in bed feeling as if electrical shocks were shooting through my body. I'd jerk myself awake, then drift off again. I'd either experience the electrical shock again or feel as if I were dying. I can't quite explain the sensation, but I felt that if I let myself fall asleep, I'd die.

I'm not sure why I struggled through these sensations, because at times I begged God to take me home anyway. When it felt as if I were going to die, I'd get quite scared. I don't think I feared death itself as much as the awful feeling that would overcome me. It's difficult to describe. At times, I'd compare the sensation to that of drowning or suffocating.

. . . I begged God to take me home anyway. When it felt as if I were going to die, I'd get quite scared . . . At times, I'd compare the feeling to that of drowning or suffocating.

The only relief I had to get through the night was to soak in the tub for relaxation. Then I could succumb to sleep in the tub without a problem. When I woke up in the bathtub, I got out and returned to bed to sleep.

At times, I slept in the tub more than in my bed. Luckily, we had a lovely soaking tub, a gift from my husband and the Lord. On the wall over the tub, was a small, flat-screen television. It was a very thoughtful gift from my son, Eric, which he purchased after he graduated from college and started his new career. I loved spending time in that tub for many reasons. It generally helped with the pain, and I could relax easier there than in a bed and fall asleep sooner.

Changes in barometric pressure were quite difficult for me. I often felt as if the air pressure around me was pressing in hard on my body and causing me pain. It was as if large, steel bands were wrapped around my legs, and gradually getting tighter and tighter. When I had my limbs under the bathwater, however, I sensed a more stabilized pressure against my legs. The sensation was as if the bands were loosening.

The most difficult nights for me were when the wind was blowing enough to rattle the house, or a new weather system came through, or the barometric pressure shifted. During these nights, almost nothing helped relieve my pain and the pressure on my body that I felt. Those nights, I spent nearly the entire night in the bathtub. Often I'd spend the next day in the tub also.

There was a time when the pain was especially bad and I didn't handle the noise and activity of our children well. I asked them several times to be quieter; however, I ended up being the one sent to my room! Darryl intervened and said, "Karen, maybe you better go to your room because they can't be any quieter than they are now." I went upstairs to get away from the commotion.

After that, I learned to go to my room when I was overwhelmed. My children knew they were always welcome to visit me there. My bedroom was my haven where I hid away from the commotion, yet I treasured the visits from my kids.

I reflect on those times and am reminded that Darryl was my true hero. He was the kids' hero too. They learned to know when I needed to retreat from them and rest. They were respectful of the time I needed to be alone.

Ashley arrived home from school some afternoons and would lie in bed with me, sharing the highlights of her day. If I were in the tub, she'd come and sit by the door on the carpet and talk to me. Those were some of my favorite times with her. I also relished the times when Graham would slip into bed next to me and talk for a while.

My lack of strength is still, to this day, amazing to me. I had been a hairdresser and was quite strong. Holding a professional hairdryer in the air for most of a workday resulted in toned and muscular arms. But, with RSD, I had little strength, if any. I couldn't hold my blow dryer. Most items I picked up felt heavier to me than they were. I've since picked up things that at one time would have been impossible or difficult for me to lift, only to surprise myself at the ease of which I picked them up.

One such item I remember as challenging to lift was Eric's college art portfolio. At the time, I couldn't even lift it from the ground. I was amazed that he was strong enough to haul it around to job interviews. I realize now that it possibly was not as heavy as I'd thought at the time. I had no clue of its actual weight. My perception of its weight was due to my lack of strength.

I suffered greatly during the course of my illness because I could no longer be a social person. I'd always enjoyed talking to and being with people. I was always up for a party, often helping to plan and execute the event. Suddenly, I was hit with the pain in my wrists and as my pain worsened, I had lost my interest in being sociable.

> *I suffered greatly during the course of my illness*
> *because I could no longer be a social person. I had*
> *always enjoyed talking to and being with people . . .*
> *I had lost my interest in being social.*

I first noticed my lack of interest in hanging out with people in the early days of my illness; I just didn't want to be around people. One of my dear friends and her husband were moving away. We were invited to a going-away party for them.

We prepared food to take and were in front of the home where the party was located. I just couldn't go in. I was anxious and felt sick to my stomach. I sent the food item in with Darryl with my regrets to the hostess and guests of honor. We turned around and went home.

Our parents were quite helpful during those years. They were in their late sixties and early seventies when I was stricken with RSD. When I was healed, they were, of course, eighteen years older. My mom did so much for us during those years, pitching in to assist, as necessary. I believe all four of our parents enjoyed helping at times, taking me for treatments, tests, or doctor appointments.

I shared earlier about the adrenaline rushes I experienced during my illness. When these occurred, I could accomplish many things. During these times where I exhibited energy and high levels of activity, some people questioned if I genuinely had an illness. I usually appeared fine on the outside. But, RSD, as other pain diseases, is frequently referred to as an "invisible disability." Some people could look at me and know I was indeed in pain. I so much appreciated the people who could recognize and acknowledge my pain.

. . . people could look at me and know I was indeed in pain. I so much appreciated the people who could recognize and acknowledge my pain.

God was very gracious to me in the big scheme of things. Other RSD patients suffered much more than I did. The disease brings many symptoms, and, for each patient, the combination of symptoms can differ. For example, some RSD sufferers report feeling an intense "heat" sensation, as if hot coals are being poured over their affected limb or limbs. I, on the other hand, only experienced that sensation for just a short time, which was certainly enough for me.

It was a blessing that I was on the low end of the spectrum of RSD. I was diagnosed with a "mild" case. Of course, as I was living through the suffering, it didn't seem mild. This diagnosis was amazing to us as a family because of the profound changes this "mild case" made to our lives. Even though the medical professionals who treated me said my case was mild, our lives were totally changed.

I cannot imagine what other RSD sufferers endure if their cases are considered more significant than mine. It could be that my pain was minimized because my friend, Carol, had given me such great advice, which I followed. When I first began suffering from the pain, she urged me not to do anything I didn't *have* to do. She begged me to save my energy and the use of my hands for what I *needed* to do. I gave up driving, hobbies, ministry, cleaning, and grocery shopping in that first year. I also was limited in the cooking I could do but helped as much as I could. Overall, I struggled to take care of my family.

As I received treatment, medications, and physical therapy, I was able to increase my activity levels. During the last few years of my illness, we finally learned the balance between me doing too much, which caused pain, and doing too little, which resulted in swollen and stiff limbs and caused the pain to increase.

I must say that even though those years were difficult, we made the most of our time the best we could. God gave us many blessings too. I can't recall all of them because they occurred so many years ago; however, I do remember some. Even though our life, in general, was tough day in and day out, I was able to do some things—things that were indeed worth paying the price of any pain that may result.

Thanks to Darryl's job, in the early days of my pain, I was able to join him in traveling to many places, including England, Northern Ireland, and the Republic of Ireland. I'm grateful that I had enough stamina to go with my husband. We made some fabulous memories together.

Our family moved three times during those years. I found myself with enough energy and zeal to set up our household; not always performing the best job, but certainly participating. I also assisted with the remodel of our house in Pittsburgh. I removed wallpaper, cleaned, and painted. Then, I'd crash for a week or two until I made myself get up and begin again.

There was a time, too, when I was actually thankful that my illness kept me at home so much. I was more available to my kids. As my abilities increased, I'd often stand at the kitchen counter cooking or cleaning up, and Eric would stand next to me to talk.

. . . I was actually thankful that my illness kept me home so much. I was more available to my kids . . .

I realized that if I were well, I probably wouldn't have been quite as available to my children. I would've been my typical, busy self, on the phone, running errands, volunteering at church and school, or crafting.

During my illness, I believe I was also more available to my husband, even though Darryl often traveled for work. When he was away, I spoke with him by phone, sometimes talking more than we did when he was home. Of course, phone conversations alone were not ideal. I was often the parent who was home and offering direction and advice. We were grateful that at least one of us was always home as the kids were growing up.

I feel very blessed that God used the stressful and challenging season of my illness to produce two incredible young men and a fabulous young woman. I am quite proud to call them my own. My sickness was part of their lives—even though they did not choose it—from their childhoods into their adulthoods. When I was diagnosed, Ashley was 9, Graham was 11, and Eric was 12. God healed me when they were 27, 29, and 30, respectively.

Those were not easy years for our family, but they shaped who we are today. For that, I am grateful. I, too, have grown through the process. Thankfully, I am not the same person I was in 1993 before my illness engulfed me.

I could be bitter and regret the years that I suffered and saw our family dynamic change dramatically. Our kids missed out on family activities that we would typically have done together. But I know God Almighty allowed this season in our lives. He used it in my life for His glory and my good, as well as in the lives of my husband, children, my parents, and Darryl's parents.

I believe that what God allows, He uses to strengthen and shape us into the men and women He wants us to be. I must also claim this promise for our children instead of questioning why I, and they, suffered so much for so long.

Nothing was the same after RSD invaded our lives. Yet somehow God used it for our good. Over the years, we witnessed the promises of God manifested in other aspects of our lives too—whether an illness, trauma, or loss, God always uses the situation or event for our good. We cling to this beautiful promise: "And we know that in all things God works for the good of those who love him, who have been called according to his purpose." (Romans 8: 28)

Some may say that this verse is overused or hurtful to those who suffer; but I've suffered much and still believe this to be solid truth. And, if I love God who made me, then I can accept His word as a healing balm to my heart.

CHAPTER 10

WEEDING THROUGH THE MESS I'D MADE

S oon after my RSD diagnosis, we moved from the Allentown area to Harleysville, about forty-five minutes away from all our friends. The move resulted in me having a tough time making new friends. I wouldn't ask anyone to go anywhere with me, such as to the mall, because they would've had to push me in a wheelchair. I gained a few new friends, but not many.

I tried to get involved in our new church but was failing at it. I was attempting to find my niche in my own strength, not leaning on God. I produced a monthly church newsletter for a couple of years. This proved to be a good outlet for me because it was something I could do from home, at any time of the day or night, when I felt up to it.

A friend helped me with the newsletter when it was time to go to press. We were often pressured to get it printed on time for Sunday's distribution because I was always doing things at the last minute. One week, I was short with my friend because of my time crunch and I insisted we do things my way.

I certainly had offended her in that moment. Although she never confronted me, I'm not sure I would have listened to her anyway. She took me before the elders, my husband, and her husband, outlining her grievances against me in a letter that she read to the group. I was stunned. My husband and the elders were surprised by her assessment of me.

I sometimes wonder what would have transpired and how much grief I could have avoided if I'd gone to the Lord after that meeting and asked Him to search my soul. I never thought to ask Him if there were "any wicked way in me." I just continued to nurse my hurt feelings and played the injured party. I'm so sorry for having hurt her so much. I'm also regretful that I held on to my own negative emotions for so long.

This event possibly spurned my downward slope into self-pity, bitterness, and pride. My pride was already a problem, or I would have reacted differently at the time of my friend's accusations. I just hate the nastiness of pride. God gently tried to convict me of my pride, yet somehow I convinced myself that I wasn't really prideful.

Many passages of scripture describe pride and its destructiveness to people as well as those around them. I've learned that God is serious about the believer's need to confess his or her pride. Proverbs 11:2 is clear: "When pride comes, then comes disgrace, but with humility comes wisdom." And "A fool's mouth lashes out with pride, but the lips of the wise protect them." (Proverbs 14:3)

Although I believed I'd trusted God's will for my life for the first sixteen years that I suffered from RSD, I did not draw close to Him for strength and comfort. At first, my excuse was that I was in such bad shape physically and emotionally that I couldn't hold my Bible. At that time, we didn't have electronic versions of the Bible that I could have used.

I did not draw close to Him for strength and comfort. At first, my excuse was that I was in such bad shape physically and emotionally that I couldn't hold my Bible.

When I finally could hold a book again, I didn't go back to reading my Bible. My excuse was that my Bible was just too heavy. Still, I could have found a smaller copy, and I could have admitted that reading it should have been the most important thing.

By the time the pain began, I'd been "doing the work of the Lord" for a long time without truly walking with Him or abiding in Him. All I tried to accomplish was in my own strength. If I'd truly been seeking Him and abiding in Him when the pain came, I would have fared much better. After I was afflicted with the pain, I wish I had turned to the Lord in prayer or music, or even listened to scripture read aloud to me, but I didn't.

Reading non-fiction books also was just as difficult because I just didn't have the mental capacity at the time to process what I was reading. When I completed a chapter or a book, it was as if I'd not read the book at all. I just couldn't recall the content.

I withdrew into inspirational fictional books—books that didn't take any thought nor presented a need for me to remember important information. My doctor was quite pleased that I found a way to cope with the pain by reading instead of lying on the couch crying, as many RSD patients do.

I joined two book clubs for $20 a month, which netted me eight books a month. These books didn't last all month. Sometimes I could read all of them within two weeks if I weren't busy. When Ashley went to college, our budget demanded that all "extra spending" be halted. I gave up my book clubs. Since I had difficulty processing and remembering what I'd read, this was no problem. I just re-read the books I already had in my collection. I had them organized by authors and the order they were written. They had become my friends.

After some time had passed, I'd often remember a storyline and go and search for it in a particular book. When we moved back to North Wales from Pittsburgh, I donated the collection. I didn't feel I needed the books any longer. I still miss them sometimes, but there are none I'd now want to re-read. This is an encouragement to me because I am no longer tied to the books that helped me get through so much pain.

I justified in my mind why I needed to read those works of fiction. After all, they contained scripture, and usually someone came to know the Lord as Savior. The storylines also included women who endured tough situations and leaned on the Lord. So, there I was, trying to justify why I could spend so many hours reading these books.

Eventually, I realized that books were also a detriment to me. I'd closely read and analyzed the conflicts the main character had with her loved one. I'd project those thoughts onto my situation—my husband and our family. My projections had to do with how I was dealing at the time with the fiery darts of the enemy—darts that women especially are so particularly good at entertaining. When I entertained those negative thoughts, I saw many negative associations between my life and the lives of the characters in the books.

I still must constantly remind myself that many of my thoughts were not of the Lord nor pleasing to Him. Even if the books seemed uplifting at the time, I used them as a substitute for interacting with God. I became as dry as a dried-up creek bed. Have you ever seen a picture of a creek bed, or even just a dirt landscape, where water had once been? The ground eventually dries up and cracks. That's what I believe my soul was like. Just wasted ground.

> *I became as dry as a dried-up creek bed . . .*
> *That's what I believe my soul was like. Just like*
> *wasted ground.*

I had no joy. I didn't feel anything when I was at church. I was not sensing the Holy Spirit's direction. I'm unsure if I could have gotten myself out of that dry and barren place any sooner than I did.

The dry creek bed of my soul mirrored a beautiful garden that had not been watered nor received rain in a long time. The weeds (sin) that I left unaddressed were not going to budge without the soil of my soul receiving water.

Just how did I arrive at this place? I ignored many years of sin and neglected my relationship with the Lord even before I got physically sick. The fact was, I was also spiritually sick.

The weeds of sin in the garden of my life began early on and progressed as time passed. I was blind to or ignored my sin, as I often did, and still do, just as I ignore the weeds in my garden.

What I really needed was to confess my sin. I have often thought of sin as weeds in a garden. You know how in spring when the weeds start to come up they are few and far between? If you don't start removing them as soon as you see them, you end up with a mess. And if you delay in taking care of the chaos or avoid it all together, the weeds begin to choke out the beauty in the garden.

What I really needed was to confess my sin. I have often thought of sin as weeds in a garden . . . If you don't start removing them as soon as you see them, you end up with a mess.

Sin is like that in our lives. If we don't confess, truly confess, and repent of sin as we live each day, we end up with a messed up life. All the good we want to do for the Lord gets choked out by sin. Sometimes there are weeds (sin) that we might not pull when we first see them, believing they will be too hard to re-move at the moment. So, we let them go and forget about them; yet, even if they are right before us, we can easily ignore them. At least, that's how I react to weeds—and sin.

But I knew I must "confess my iniquity because I was troubled by my sin," as Psalm 38:18 admonishes. Attempts to hide sin from God are never the answer, according to Proverbs 28:13. "Whoever conceals their sins does not prosper, but the one who confesses and renounces them finds mercy."

I knew confession would soon be my friend. Psalm 32:5 was yet another reminder of where I was in my standing before the Lord: "Then I acknowledged my sin to you and did not cover up my iniquity. I said, 'I will confess my transgressions to the Lord.' And you forgave the guilt of my sin."

The gardens outside my windows take work. They need weeding, pruning, and watering. If I allow them to go without the proper attention, eventually I must overhaul them. On our property, we have gardens at all levels of maturity and need. Recently, one garden seemed to be an example of where I found myself—in dire need of an overhaul.

I spent a long day on my knees in that garden, working diligently to prune and weed, sometimes tearing out plants because they were beyond saving. I persevered in my garden and weeded like a maniac. I got my garden looking beautiful again.

However, soon after, I saw that I didn't get out all the roots. They were still visible! Sadly, just as in the Christian life, if we do not confess our sin regularly, the deeply rooted weeds return in full force.

I saw that I didn't get out all the roots. They were still visible! Sadly, just as in the Christian life, if we do not confess our sin regularly, the deeply rooted weeds return in full force.

My weed of pride was a huge part of the problem. I pictured it as having a deep-seated root, making it difficult to retrieve from dry and compacted land. However, God's Word contains this wonderful promise: "If we confess our sins, he is faithful and just and will forgive us our sins and purify us from all unrighteousness." (I John 1:9)

The overhaul on my soul's garden, full of weeds, took much longer than the garden outside my window took me to beautify. God's Holy Spirit, my Gardener, gently nurtured me. It took the next year and a half to get me to the point in my walk with Him that we could eradicate the weeds. God spent time gently sprinkling my soul with truth—beautiful truth that eventually soaked into that dry soul and revived it.

In addition, my new friends in Pittsburgh did not know just how much they played a positive role in my new season. They ministered to me greatly, living out Ephesians 5:19, which states, "speaking to one another with psalms, hymns, and songs from the Spirit. Sing and make music from your heart to the Lord."

CHAPTER 11

SLIPPING FURTHER INTO DEPRESSION

D
ad passed away in April 2003, after two exceedingly difficult months of declining health. During this time, I had the privilege of helping my mom with his care. It was a really tough time, but one I wouldn't change for anything. Mom, at 83, was his primary caregiver. I'd spend a week or so helping out, then travel the forty-five minutes back home for a few days to recover before returning to help again.

This time with Dad was especially sweet, because I finally had a dad who loved God, and Dad was looking forward to going home to heaven. Dad had accepted Christ as a young boy of eleven. Even so, he lived a long life fighting against the surrender of his will to God's. About six months before he died, he returned to the Lord.

For that short while between his coming back to faith and those last months, my dad was the one who wanted to say grace at dinner. This small act doesn't seem very telling, yet for my dad it said everything! Just before he slipped into a coma in those last few days, he spoke to mom and me individually, sharing his love for us.

I was outside for a few minutes as Dad recited the Lord's Prayer with Mom. Then I came in and he talked to me about taking care of mom, the goodness of the Lord, and being ready to go home. I thanked him for being such a wonderful grandpop to our children. He was as fantastic a grandpop as he could have been and taught his grandchildren very much.

When our children were young, my parents alternated with Darryl's parents to watch the kids when we'd go away with the teens from our church. We'd return home to stories of how Dad took things apart, such as tape recorders, cassettes, and other household items, just so the kids could be amazed at how things worked. It was magical!

Dad was always on a different sleeping cycle from the rest of us. Because of that, a family tradition was birthed. By the time Dad ate breakfast around midmorning, his toddler grandchildren who were visiting would be getting hungry again, since they'd eaten much earlier.

Each of the children, except one, without knowing the others had done this, had the privilege of sitting with Grandpop while he ate his breakfast. They all wanted to share his breakfast of bacon and eggs, and each one insisted that it had to be the very food on Dad's plate. Mom prepared a dish for Dad with more food on it than he typically had for breakfast. Sharing Grandpop's breakfast was a rite of passage for his grandchildren.

Losing dad was quite difficult for our family. When he finally passed into Glory, I did a fist pump in the air because I was elated for him and knew he was so ready to go. Only my selfishness would have wanted him to stay here longer.

Even so, while I grieved, I was at peace about losing him. But I didn't allow myself to truly grieve his passing.

Only three months later, we lost our niece Kerry, the precious one with spina bifida. As she was growing up, she was never told she couldn't do things. She was encouraged to try whatever she wanted. She received a walker at a young age, and then as she progressed with the walkers, was later fitted with crutches.

Although the physical therapists didn't think she'd be able to walk far with crutches, as she was learning to use them, her therapist coached her, backing down the hall facing her. We were all amazed as to how quickly Kerry learned to walk with crutches. Once I watched her walk with the crutches— one of them rarely touched the ground because she had learned to get about so quickly.

She was wheelchair-bound by the end of her life, but she didn't allow her physical hindrances to hold her back from what she wanted to experience. Kerry accomplished more in her short life than most kids ever do. During her last week, before she went into the hospital, she even served as a sports camp counselor for younger medically fragile children.

She had also been on a traveling wheelchair basketball team and was later the team manager. She was also attending college while living at home with her parents. They had the privilege of watching her fall in love. An engagement was on the horizon. She then spent the last few months of her life traveling.

It almost appears, as we reflect, that my sweet niece may have been checking off items from her bucket list. She even had plans to come to visit my parents and my family, but Dad died before her visit. She was able to be at his funeral, though.

She stayed with our family several weeks after her family left. During that sweet time, she and I went shopping, she in her wheelchair and me in the store's riding buggy. She was quick in getting around; I couldn't keep up with her.

Little did we know that would be our last visit. Just two months later, she was in the hospital in Albuquerque. My mom and I went to see her. We stayed until she passed away and were there for her funeral. I am so thankful for being able to be with Kerry and my family as we once again said goodbye to a beloved family member.

After these two back-to-back funerals, I began to go downhill emotionally. I got sad, angry, bitter, and even more unforgiving. I was letting any and all slight offenses eat away at me.

We as Christians are taught to forgive, and not just once. "Then Peter came to Jesus and asked, "Lord, how many times shall I forgive my brother or sister who sins against me? Up to seven times?" Jesus answered, "I tell you, not seven times, but seventy-seven times." (Matthew 18:21-22)

One of the things I forgot to practice was not letting slight offenses bother me by letting go of the offenses and forgiving the offender.

I slipped further and further downhill into depression and felt more and more sorry for myself. Then, I felt slighted by a couple of people in our church. Instead of forgiving them and letting it go, I rehearsed the offenses both in my mind and verbally with my husband.

I felt slighted by a couple of people in our church.
Instead of forgiving them and letting it go, I
rehearsed the offenses both in my mind and verbally
with my husband.

I took offense one Sunday when I learned about something from the pulpit that really stung. I walked out, never to go back again. After we left that church, I had trouble wanting to be vulnerable with another church family. We "shopped around" and then found a large church where we appreciated the teaching, yet we could walk in and out of the doors without worrying about anyone trying to befriend us.

That's a sad commentary to describe a church. We went to that church for almost four years. The only people we talked to were a few who we knew from elsewhere. I don't think anyone at that church ever greeted us nor asked anything about us. No one ever personally invited us to any activities.

In the church's defense, it was full of Sunday morning believers as well as "seekers." I was just as guilty. I never talked to anyone whom I didn't know. Since then, I've learned not to stand around at a church waiting for someone to reach out to me. Who am I to think that others need to be the first to talk to me?

I finally became mature enough spiritually to realize that the God who loves me made me the way I am. I then had ammunition against that lie. I began smiling and greeting everyone at church. I've witnessed people open up to me just because I made an effort first to befriend them. I believe that people come to church genuinely hoping that someone will approach them with a smile, a hug, or a word of encouragement.

During those dark years of depression, I didn't have many friends. I'd learned to be more socially bold at church, I didn't have many friends. Things inside of me were tearing me apart. I needed someone to talk to about what was going on. I didn't have a girlfriend.

I should have sought out a counselor, but just couldn't get myself to go to one. I'd gotten the idea stuck in my head that Christians shouldn't need counseling. I don't know where I got this notion since biblical counseling provides wisdom. However, God's word is clear that biblical advice is wise, as stated in Proverbs 19:20: "Listen to advice and accept discipline, and at the end you will be counted among the wise."

Deep down inside, I knew counseling would benefit me. I could have saved myself much grief had I shared my inner struggles with a qualified professional. Maybe this person could have helped me weed my garden a lot more quickly!

Initially, I was determined not to seek help because I knew that if I talked about some of my struggles, my mask would eventually fall off. I thought I'd no longer be able to make people think I was a good Christian. Seeking godly counsel would have been far better than slipping into the cesspool of my mind. Now, as a sincere and consistent seeker of His will and the kingdom of God, I can usually turn over whatever it is that eats at me much more quickly. This is because I've finally learned to abide in Him.

Forgiveness also is much easier for me now. When Satan tries to take my mind back to things in the past, I know to stop dwelling on these things. With God, all things are new. His mercies are new every morning! I know that leaving my burdens with the Lord is the best option for me. Forgiveness, like exercise, must occur over and over until, finally, the process of forgiving comes without struggle.

Similarly, I hope that one day my bike riding will become better with practice. Each time I ride, it's getting easier, but I am a long way off of where I'd like to be. My bike riding goal at this time in my life is to climb the hill of our street (look hard or you might miss that it's a hill) and be able to climb the three steps up into our house without having wobbly legs! Maybe I should first walk around the yard a bit before climbing the steps.

How grateful we can be to know that we do not need to arrive at church with placards hanging around our necks announcing our sin. I'm thankful to have realized that we, as believers in Jesus, should not deny that we have sin in our lives. It's okay for others to see that we have imperfections.

If we attempt to make others believe that we are perfect, we will fail. We are not perfect. We cannot be perfect. Sometimes, I think we're hard on struggling Christians who believe that this life is just too hard. Like me, we soon are convinced that we can make ourselves look like the perfect Christian on the outside, but the weeds of our internal garden are long overdue for pulling!

We moved into our current home in 2006. We only lived there for eighteen months, then moved to Pittsburgh and rented out the house. We moved back into it in 2013.

The eighteen months that we first lived there was the darkest of seasons for me. At times, I wondered if the house was demon-possessed. I experienced a considerable amount of overwhelming oppression. It may have been demons who were sent to torment me; but, more than likely, the oppression I experienced was probably a result of all the ugly weeds that had overtaken my internal garden. I was not allowing God, my Gardener, into my daily life.

So, with my soul so very dry and weed-choked, my life and mind were in such a dark place. I didn't entertain the act of committing suicide, but the thought that floated through my mind was, "Oh, my family would be so much better off without me."

During those first months in the house, I cried out to God to take me home. I still had my faith and knew that life in heaven would be so much better than life on earth. Yet, I was a bitter, angry, miserable woman who was choking on all the weeds in her garden. I must have been a pretty awful person to be around at that time. I didn't like myself very much, so why would anyone else want to be around such a miserable person?

Few people went out of their way to be my friend. We had a few friends, and we are still close to one couple, the Walshes, who befriended us. I would have to say that without Darryl along, I didn't spend much time with friends. Nor did I feel as if my family wanted to be around me. I'm unsure how much of this negative feeling was real. It's possible that my negativity was a symptom of where I was spiritually and emotionally. Or, it could have been that I was entertaining the thoughts that the enemy was throwing my way.

"Oh, Lord! Take me home," I pleaded. I remember being jealous of a man we knew who died at a young age. I attended his funeral, which was quite a journey from home. I drove about an hour to meet some old friends and then we drove together another two hours. By the time I arrived at the funeral, I was in quite a bit of physical pain. I sat there, staring at his casket, wishing it were me, not he who was with God.

I can't look back on the darkness I endured with regret. However, I wish there were things that I knew then that I know now. I must trust that my God knows best.

CHAPTER 12

MY JOURNEY BACK
TO GOD

God was leading me on a personal journey back to Himself. As I think about my spiritual revival and look back over the past years, I see that my journey began in the summer of 2007 when Darryl was presented with a new job.

We witnessed how God worked in our lives at that time with both the new job and a subsequent move to Pittsburgh. I'd never lived anywhere other than the Philadelphia area, yet I was excited about the idea of living elsewhere.

We didn't have much time to get our house ready for sale. We were still rather partial to the house because we'd only owned it for a year and a half. The housing market was plummeting, so we put the house up for rent and posted a sign on the lawn. Just three days later, we had a check in our hands and a renter ready to move in.

We looked at many types of houses, condos, and apartments in our new city of Pittsburgh. However, the moment I first walked around to see the back of one particular house, I knew Darryl would want it. He'd always wanted a wooded lot. The house was perfect for us and we made the purchase.

We moved in, adopted an adorable Bichon Frisé named Spencer, remodeled the kitchen, and painted the exterior. We also located a new church home. We were ready to begin our new life.

We'd purchased a home large enough for visitors, mostly thinking of our children and our parents. It would be just the two of us for the time being. Ashley was living in Chicago; Graham and Eric were living in the Philadelphia area.

Not long after our kitchen remodel, I received a call from Ashley. Her best friend from high school, who had stayed with us many weekends, had a need. Ashley had seen us meet these types of needs before inviting people into our home to stay. So, this need was an easy one.

Ashley's friend, Kelly, was expecting her first baby. Kelly's husband was going into the Air Force to pursue a new career. Ashley asked if Kelly and the baby could live with us while Simeon was in boot camp. What a blessing it was for all of us. I believe, too, that the home God had led us to was also God's provision for them.

Kelly and the baby lived with us seven months from Thanksgiving 2008 until the following May. Kelly's husband also lived with us for two months before he left for boot camp.

Darryl and I ate well those months. The planning, shopping, and cooking of meals were all exceedingly difficult for me. On our own, we often ate canned soup because it was an easy alternative.

When Kelly moved in, we made a deal: I watched baby Josiah while she went grocery shopping and planned our meals. She loved this arrangement, enjoyed shopping, and treasured time by herself. Likewise, I was enjoying time alone with her precious baby.

As Kelly prepared dinner, I'd lie on the floor of the family room and play with the baby. We all reaped the benefits of Kelly's excellent cooking skills. Her talent and willingness filled a great need, and she enjoyed being helpful.

I also began my journey of healing emotionally. This journey included fostering other Bichons, like our precious Spencer, which also aided in my healing. This was a fun adventure, sometimes grueling, yet enjoyable. I met new people and experienced ways to get beyond my own needs. After a year, however, I had to relinquish my love of fostering dogs; my energy level was depleted. But we enjoyed our own fluffy white dog for many more years.

The activities in this new home were part of God's plan to bring me back to Him. I was beginning to encounter a spiritual revival within my heart. But I didn't change from the bitter and miserable woman that I was overnight. My transformation was a gradual shifting of my attitude, which occurred partly because of the recent change in lifestyle and our surroundings.

I was beginning to encounter a spiritual revival within my heart. But I didn't change from the bitter and miserable woman that I was overnight.

The church we joined played a huge part in my journey. I'd never experienced a church quite as loving, welcoming, and inclusive as this church. We walked in the doors, and the people of that wonderful church loved me back to the Lord.

From the time we started attending, a kind couple took it upon themselves to pray for me. I had told them early on about my RSD. Each Sunday that I went to church, the husband greeted me with great joy and said, "Karen, I'm so happy to see you. I prayed this morning that you would make it today." I'm convinced that their prayers for me to attend church were answered. Because I knew he was praying for me and looking for me, I would push myself to go. Someone wanted me.

Another result of this man's prayers was that I now saw the need to improve my church attendance. In early 2010, God convicted me of my willingness to let church attendance to be optional. I had somehow slipped into allowing my discomfort of being around people, my pain, my nausea, and my poor sleep habits to keep me at home.

Before I was ill, I was in the habit of attending church regularly. I was raised to attend church every Sunday, and Darryl and I had done the same with our children. Sadly, going to church had become a rote habit by the time I fell ill. I'm unsure if I'd ever attended church for the right reason of worshiping my God.

When I first suffered from RSD, I went to church in terrible pain. I didn't allow my pain to keep me home, however. Then in 1995, a year after my diagnosis, we moved about forty-five minutes away. We found another church, but I began to develop a litany of excuses to miss church.

In Pittsburgh, I was again attending regularly by the time God convicted me. His conviction helped me realize how I'd slipped away and that I needed to change my attitude about "why" I go to church. I needed to go in obedience to Him; however, I still didn't attend because I desired to worship God.

That spring, I read a book about relationships titled, *The Emotionally Destructive Relationship*, by Leslie Vernick. I was struck by how destructive I am in relationships. Then something the author wrote made me realize that God really loves me. Yes! He loves me! This simple revelation was life-changing for me.

I'd always taught my children that Jesus loved them. And yes, I knew He loved me. But now, I truly embraced the fact that God loves me. He even liked who I was because He created me. I realized at that moment that His love and acceptance were all I needed.

I cried out to this Lord who loved me so much. He met me right where I was. He didn't ask me to clean up my act first before He could help me. No, He began working in my life right then and there.

My dried-up soul took much work to be revived. Just as a dry creek bed needs to be revived gradually by the application of water, my soul needed to be watered with God's truth. I needed, more than anything, a slow, continuous application of truth.

My dried-up soul took much work to be revived.
Just as a dry creek bed needs to be revived
gradually by the application of water, my soul
needed to be watered with God's truth.

:ied to drench myself in God's Word, it would have
ht off of me. What I needed was a steady, daily, and
cons:... i watering, allowing His truth to soak into me and
change me on the inside.

Amazingly, God began to send revival into my heart
through verses and songs I saw and heard through my friends'
posts on social media. I also found a Christian radio station and
had it on almost always. God began whispering to me through
the music and the stories.

I also posted scripture on my mirror to remind me of the
truths God was teaching me. One verse that had a permanent
place on my mirror that summer of 2010 was Psalm 63:1:
"You, God, are my God, earnestly I seek you; I thirst for you,
my whole being longs for you, in a dry and parched land where
there is no water."

God used various avenues to sprinkle truth into my dry land
and revive me. He taught me and guided me along the way. My
soul became a beautiful picture of a steady and consistent rain
falling on the parched creek bed of my life.

God used various avenues to sprinkle truth into my
dry land and revive me. He taught me and guided
me along the way.

That fall, I joined a Bible study with several women from different churches. These women taught me again to pray diligently
and seek God. I began to grow in the Lord and mature in my faith.
God was leading me on a two-year long revival up a mountain.

In January 2011, I had an appointment with my pain management psychiatrist back in Philadelphia. I was early and had

some time to kill. I went for a walk nearby and saw a Christian bookstore.

As I wandered into the store and strolled around, a book caught my eye. It had an eye-catching cover. I have no idea why except the prompting of the Holy Spirit led me to pick up that book. I headed to the counter to make a purchase—a purchase of a book about biblical fasting.

> *. . . a book caught my eye. It had an eye-catching cover. I have no idea why except the prompting of the Holy Spirit led me to pick up that book . . . a book about biblical fasting.*

I quickly read the book, focusing intently on the contents regarding fasting. I'd never fasted, and with all the scripture regarding fasting, I was dumbfounded as to how I could have reached my age without ever fasting. I had thought many times that I needed to fast, but excuses got in the way.

Fasting is for our benefit and not for God's benefit. And spiritual fasting must be specific and intentional. I'd read about fasting but had not heard of anyone in my Christian circles talk about doing a fast. God waited to urge me to fast when I was genuinely ready to fast out of obedience.

In one month's time, I had bought a book on fasting, listened to an online sermon about fasting, and later listened to a message on fasting from our pastor. It was now time to fast.

> *In one month's time, I had bought a book on fasting, listened to an online sermon about fasting, and later listened to a message on fasting from our pastor. It was now time to fast.*

My first fast was the "Daniel fast" as outlined in the book. I found that I was able to do it and even enjoyed giving up something for my Lord. I didn't eat meat, sugar, caffeine, and other foods for 21 consecutive days. This period was a significant time of learning for me.

I became obsessed, however, with the process of fasting and not with God's goal for me during my time of fasting. I was caught up in making sure everything I bought was sugar-free. Surely if I used pasta sauce containing sugar, God would consider my fast null and void. So, I didn't put any food in my mouth without first studying labels. I don't believe it was wrong to want to "do it right." But when the desire to do right supersedes doing "as unto the Lord," that's when it's a wrong motive.

In those days, I was still ill. A total fast, therefore, would have proven dangerous with all the medications I took. However, I felt I could handle the Daniel fast, which I strictly followed. Doing so gave me a feeling of "yes, I can do this!"

I believe spiritual fasting must be Spirit-led for a specific reason or a season when a church, nation, or spiritual leader calls for everyone to fast and pray over a specific need. I had never been part of such a call to fast.

Matthew 6, verses 16-18, describe the significance of fasting in the early church: "When you fast, do not look somber as the hypocrites do, for they disfigure their faces to show others they are fasting. Truly I tell you, they have received their reward in full. But when you fast, put oil on your head and wash your face, so that it will not be obvious to others that you are fasting, but only to your Father, who is unseen; and your Father, who sees what is done in secret, will reward you."

The Bible warns us that fasting is to be all about seeking God. It isn't about getting what we want; it's aligning ourselves with the will of God in our lives.

The Bible warns us that fasting is to be all about seeking God. It isn't about getting what we want; it's aligning ourselves with the will of God in our lives.

We must look at how Christians before us benefitted from praying and fasting. Even our forefathers asked the country to fast and pray, and our great, God-fearing nation was born through those prayers. Abraham Lincoln and others called for the American people to fast and pray.

It's interesting how the Holy Spirit guides us, sometimes subtly or not so subtly, to follow His promptings. I'm grateful for the timing of fasting in my life. It was a matter of obedience for me. God used this fasting experience as part of my continued story of spiritual revival.

That spring, in 2011, I was in a good place. I was walking with the Lord. I was happy. I was doing somewhat well with RSD, managing my daily activities and pain levels. I had no idea, however, what would be coming my way in the following year.

I love this passage from Hosea 6:1-3, which truly depicted my journey: "Come, let us return to the LORD. He has torn us to pieces but he will heal us; he has injured us but he will bind up our wounds. After two days he will revive us; on the third day he will restore us, that we may live in his presence. Let us acknowledge the LORD; let us press on to acknowledge him.

As surely as the sun rises, he will appear; he will come to us like the winter rains, like the spring rains that water the Earth."

How good that we don't know what's next. I'm sure that if I knew what was coming, I would have gotten in the Lord's way. That's just my nature. Yet, when we draw near to Him, He comes to us with a deluge of blessing. And I was soon to experience such a downpour.

CHAPTER 13

PURPOSELY SEEKING HIS KINGDOM

I'll never forget sitting in my living room in the summer of 2011. Our church small group was engaged in a study and we read Matthew 6:33. Immediately, that verse stood out to me as if it had been divinely highlighted: "But seek first his kingdom and his righteousness, and all these things will be given to you as well."

I was suddenly intrigued with this verse. For the first time, it was meaningful to me. I'd never before taken it to heart. I was determined to purposely seek His Kingdom. I wasn't sure exactly what that meant; however, not realizing it, I'd already been seeking God's Kingdom for the past year, since I first begged God to revive the soil of my dry heart.

God's Kingdom is not some ethereal place somewhere that we will one day find ourselves; rather, it is a believer's state of walking in complete obedience to Him, allowing God to rule and reign. I know I will never achieve this state until He calls me home. The good news is that I can seek His Kingdom on earth by being obedient, listening to His still, small voice, and following His direction.

God's Kingdom is not some ethereal place
somewhere that we will one day find ourselves;
rather, it is a believer's state of walking in complete
obedience to Him . . .

I learned that if I first seek God's Kingdom, all the things I am worried about will be provided or given to me according to His will. I knew I must focus on the one thing I *could certainly do*—seek God's Kingdom!

As I chose to seek Him, He drew me further into His Kingdom. I learned to seek and abide. I could almost feel an overwhelming sense of love, graciousness, comfort, and joy. The flood of His blessings was covering my life. I believe the Holy Spirit orchestrated that time in my life for His purpose.

As fall progressed, my desire for television dwindled. At night, when I couldn't sleep, I'd play computer games and listen to a particular pastor's sermons that I found online. I had lost much of my Bible knowledge over the years, most of it buried behind the medicated wall of my mind.

I found myself in the middle of a crash course, desiring to restore my knowledge of God's word. This pastor certainly taught me how to put the scriptures into practice. His sermons were like arrows shot into my heart. I listened intently to his sermons; one series in particular was life-changing.

This pastor gave incredible descriptions of God, Heaven, Jesus, and the Holy Spirit. I now had so much greater awe, respect, and love for The Father, The Savior, and The Comforter who guides me. This series of messages brought about a downpour of revival and blessing in my life.

I also learned to long for heaven where I will be part of his eternal Kingdom. There, the things of earth will certainly grow strangely dim. I will then be forever consumed with my Savior, praising, and glorifying Him. Nothing else will matter anymore.

When I look back on that feeling of being consumed by the Savior the months before and after my healing, I can't imagine getting to heaven just to ask questions about my illness, events that happened in my life or to obtain answers. I doubt I'll be approaching Him to ask things about this earthly life.

I don't know many things about heaven, but I do know this: Jesus will be my all in all. My focus will be to worship and serve Him. However, for my remaining time on earth, I will continue to seek His Kingdom. His promise is to continue to work on and through me.

One particular sermon I heard from this same pastor was about sin. Just as with weeding, when the ground is dry, weeds, as well as sin, are difficult to uproot. God worked on the barren land of my soul for quite some time to ready my soil for weeding. The overhaul of my soul began.

And so, God began earnestly dealing with me and my past sin—sin that I'd not yet confessed to him. My prayers of confession up to that point were ones similar to, "forgive me for any sins I committed today." I didn't pray specifically because I couldn't face my sin. So, I tried not to think about it. But that fall, God had something else in mind for me.

I was faced with so much sin that I had never identified as such. God led me on a journey through many of my sins from years past. This spiritual exercise was the most painful, yet most productive time in my revival.

I realized that my sins of self were some of my worst. I'd not realized that my self-awareness, self-degradation, self-hatred, and internalizing negative thoughts were all sin. How could I talk that way about someone whom God had created and whom he saw as precious in his sight?

However, once I began confessing these personal sins, God Himself rooted them out! He tossed them away! Yet, at the same time, He was pointing out to me that there were other roots (sin) that I'd not pulled, or confessed, for many years.

One strong memory is when I was in church, standing during the worship time. It was the Easter after I was healed. That morning, a memory flashed in my mind—a time when I acted sinfully toward someone. I immediately confessed this memory to the Lord and continued worshipping.

These snapshot memories still pop into my mind. They come less often, but God occasionally reveals a sin that I still need to confess. Sometimes the memory is one from decades ago. Yes, it would have been much easier to confess the sin back then. However, I knew God had forgiven me long before I experienced the memory; I just needed to get right with God by confessing that I was wrong. I don't need to berate myself for my sin; instead, I must take steps to confess, forget as He forgets, and move on. In the strength He gives me through the Holy Spirit, I can do this, as I am reminded by Ephesians 3:16: "I pray that out of his glorious riches he may strengthen you with power through his Spirit in your inner being."

And then the deluge started. I was consumed with learning all the scriptural truths I had forgotten over the years. I was on a mountaintop with God. I felt as if I could understand what Moses felt up on the mountain. Consistent church attendance as a priority had been just the first step of obedience the Lord had asked of me.

I sensed God asking me to cover my head in corporate prayer and worship. I now wear a hat in church to show my obedience, respect, and submission to the Father, and also to respect my husband. The head covering is a reminder to me that I want to be obedient to the Lord in all I do, *even if I'm the only one doing so.* I must remind myself of this often, because, as a human, I still disobey.

Through all this I learned to desire and enjoy being in God's presence. I focused on going to church to worship the King of Kings. I wanted Him and Him alone to be my focus. Church was not just a place for friendly conversations, donuts, and coffee. It's primary purpose was to be a corporate gathering in a house of worship.

> *I focused on going to church to worship the King of Kings. I wanted Him and Him alone to be my focus. Church was not just a place for friendly conversations, donuts, and coffee.*

I learned that my primary motivation was to please my Lord, not to appear to be a "good Christian." To this day, I strive to obey His word and His voice because of Jesus' horrendous death on the cross for me.

I also needed to learn to obey when it comes to forgiveness, but it was not an easy thing for me. Mark 11:25 admonishes: "And when you stand praying if you hold anything against anyone, forgive them, so that your Father in heaven may forgive you your sins."

How often do we acknowledge that the Father will not forgive our sins unless we first forgive? There's no wiggle room in this admonition! Of course, the lies of Satan tell us that the person who hurt us doesn't deserve forgiveness.

Of course, the lies of Satan tell us that the person who hurt us doesn't deserve forgiveness.

God is willing to forgive anyone who comes to Him in repentance with a changed heart and the willingness to turn from sin. This truth is outlined in Acts 13:38: "Therefore, my friends, I want you to know that through Jesus, the forgiveness of sins is proclaimed to you. Through him, *everyone* who believes is set free from every sin." (emphasis added)

I was a bitter, angry woman who had held onto some things, not forgiving others for perceived or real slights. God brought me to a place of forgiveness for many people. I forgave many family members, friends, doctors, and nurses for the slights I had perceived. Yes, perceived. Most of the bitter and negative things I'd held on to probably never were reality. Letting go was very freeing!

One such grievance I held on to was the bitterness I felt for a particular church we'd been members of for about ten years. God asked me to write a letter to the staff of that church because I'd left there in a huff. He instructed me to ask them to forgive me and to state that I forgave them for the slight I'd held onto for so long. I wrote the letter, but I didn't mail it right away.

Taking things personally caused me so much pain that I could have avoided. I have been trying to "let go" of these slight offenses as I know this is God's plan for His children. He does not want us to suffer mentally over our inability to forgive.

Forgiveness is not easy. We know this to be true because we have such a difficult time forgiving. And yet, our heavenly Father will forgive us of all our sins if we repent and confess our sins.

Friend, if you are still holding on to unforgiveness, take care of it now. You might still dislike, mistrust, or expect restitution from him or her. But, for you to have a right relationship with God, you must forgive.

Forgiving was definitely one hard point of obedience the Father was asking of me. However, with my confession of sins, forgiving was quite freeing and helpful as I continued to seek His Kingdom.

CHAPTER 14

THE BLESSINGS OF PRAYER

Another area of obedience that I finally surrendered to God was my prayer life. I'd always believed in prayer, to a certain extent. I knew God would certainly answer prayer, but I didn't really expect Him to answer "big" prayers such as physical healing. Through my ordeal, I have learned to trust in the power of prayer, no matter how big or small the request.

Sometimes, even now, I take scripture for granted. Maybe this is a result of reading it many times, hearing it repeatedly from the pulpit, or not fully digesting the true meaning of the scripture. Perhaps I've forgotten God's promises and just don't practice them.

Have you ever been sick and gone to the elders of your church and asked them to anoint you with oil and pray over you? James 5:13-16 reminds us of this: "Is anyone among you in trouble? Let them pray. Is anyone happy? Let them sing songs of praise. Is anyone among you sick? Let them call the elders of the church to pray over them and anoint them with oil in the name of the Lord. And the prayer offered in faith will make the sick person well; the Lord will raise

). If they have sinned, they will be forgiven. Therefore confess your sins to each other and pray for each other so that you may be healed. The prayer of a righteous person is powerful and effective."

Many believers too often forget the admonitions outlined in these verses. So, why do we choose not to do what God's word tells us to do? Why do we doubt that our prayers will be answered?

> *So, why do we choose not to do what God's word*
> *tells us to do? Why do we doubt that our prayers*
> *will be answered?*

Until the season of my revival, if I read James 5:14, I never would have noticed how the verse mentions that the sick must go to the elders. I suffered almost eighteen years, yet I never fully comprehended the meaning of those verses, and I never knew if the first three churches we attended while I was sick even practiced anointing and praying.

In December 2011, while reading the book of James, the Holy Spirit opened my eyes to what these verses actually say—that it was *my job* to go to the elders; they were not to come to me. I was under the impression that if our church practiced this scripture, the elders would come and offer to pray for me. I was wrong. I had also never heard any of my Christian acquaintances talk about having been anointed and prayed over.

But, after the Lord opened my eyes, I asked the elders of my church to anoint me and pray for my healing. It was

Christmas Eve, 2011. They said they anoint and pray over anyone who asks it of them. So, we set a date a couple of weeks later, in January.

At that moment, I only knew that I had never asked for the elders to pray over me. I needed to obey God's word and ask them. I was not, however, asking them to pray over me for my healing. I didn't think that was possible because eighteen years earlier, God had whispered to me that He did not have healing for me now.

I later realized that Christmas Eve was not the appropriate time to ask my elders for something so important. Asking them was irrelevant to all their holiday responsibilities. They probably wouldn't even remember later that I'd asked them on such a busy day.

I talked myself into many reasons why I shouldn't follow through with the date we'd set. However, I sensed that there was a last step of obedience the Lord was asking of me before I could meet with my elders—to mail the letter I'd written earlier to my previous church regarding my apology and request for forgiveness.

Dropping the letter into the mail would have been easy. I just didn't do it. I was entertaining other negative thoughts from the enemy, including fear. What would be the response from the church leaders after they'd read my letter of apology?

Dropping the letter into the mail would have been easy. I just didn't do it. I was entertaining other negative thoughts from the enemy . . .

Even though I'd asked my elders and they'd agreed, I thought I didn't deserve for them to pray over me. After all, the letter hadn't yet been mailed, and I'd not reminded the elders of the date we'd set to meet.

A year before I asked for anointing and prayer from my elders, I shared with my ladies Bible study group that I was in terrible pain in my hips. I don't think I mentioned the pain in my back at that time because my hips were more of an issue.

I was taking Kadian because it was the only pain killer that worked well for my nerve pain. This medication gave no relief from the other pain I experienced, and the doctors found nothing "wrong" with my hips or back, so they were not treating these areas.

A couple of the ladies in my study group were elders in their churches where they practice anointing with oil. These dear women anointed me with oil and prayed over me. One woman, Sheila, also prayed for my healing from RSD. After they prayed, I said to her, "I don't believe God has healing from the RSD in my future. This (RSD) is not something that can be healed." She replied, "Karen, I believe that God *is* going to heal you."

We left our Bible study that day in the normal buzz of conversation. I didn't notice right away that my hip pain was gone, but it was! The hip pain had been somewhat intermittent; consequently, it was a few days before I realized that the pain in my hips was gone, never to come back like that again.

We left our Bible study that day in the normal buzz of conversation. I didn't notice right away that my hip pain was gone . . .

I was going to a chiropractor for my back and experienced the first relief I'd had in almost ten years. The chiropractor believed that my pelvis was misaligned, which was causing my pain. She gave me adjustments, which greatly relieved my pain. God used both the anointing prayers and the power of chiropractic to heal me of the non-RSD pain.

Just a few years ago, as I was penning this memoir, I suffered pain in my back again. I was in quite a bit of pain leading up to the time that I was to volunteer with a friend at the Operation Christmas Child shoebox processing center in Maryland in November 2016. I knew it would be a long couple of days of physical labor—organizing, boxing, and stacking. I considered not going because I wasn't sure I'd be able to stand for my entire shift.

I asked God to direct me as to whether I should go. I felt a peace about going, drove to my friend's house, and spent the night. Early the next morning we were on our way. I was in pain. I couldn't even sit comfortably; I was in constant motion, trying to avoid the pain as we traveled. We arrived and got to work.

At each shift I worked that day and the next, Operation Christmas Child staff members would stop us and ask us to join in prayer. We all stood over some of the donated shoeboxes with our hands on as many as we could touch. Someone prayed for the boxes and the children who would soon receive them.

During the first shift, I remember the staff person who prayed was also praying for the volunteer workers. She prayed that if anyone were sick or in pain, that the Lord would heal

ıt, "God, I'm going to accept that healing for my-
k pain was gone immediately! I worked for a day
thout any pain. Not all my prayers are answered
that quickly and positively, but many times I see the hand of
God work mightily in my prayers.

For a long time, I never really understood that God places
conditions on His willingness to hear our prayers. God doesn't
say He will answer everyone's prayers, for everything we request, with a "yes." Many modern-day Christians, and even
non-Christians, have arrived at the conclusion that answered
prayer means, "Yes, I'll do that for you."

*For a long time, I never really understood that
God places conditions on His willingness to
hear our prayers.*

In His sovereignty, God can answer any prayer that He
wishes, in the way that he chooses. His Word, the Bible,
tells us a few things about some guidelines we must follow for God to answer our prayers. An admonition in Isaiah
59:2, which says that our sins get in the way of answered
prayer. "But your iniquities have separated you from your
God; your sins have hidden his face from you, so that he
will not hear."

God will, however, answer anyone who calls out to him in
faith, accepting His gift of eternal life. To receive eternal life,
you must first confess and agree with God that sin is the opposite of what God wants for each of us. We must realize that the
payment for our sin is death.

Jesus took it upon Himself to bear our sin on the cross so that we would no longer be separated from God. If we accept Jesus' sacrifice and believe that He died for us, we will be saved and have eternal life. "For God did not send His son into the world to condemn the world, but to save the world through Him." (John 3:17)

Believers in Jesus must not have unconfessed sin in their lives. As followers of Jesus, we must examine ourselves as David says in Psalm 139:23-24: "Search me, God, and know my heart; test me and know my anxious thoughts. See if there is any offensive way in me and lead me in the way everlasting."

Confession of sin is a must; it is not optional. "If we confess our sins, He is faithful and just and will forgive us our sins and purify us from all unrighteousness" (1 John 1:9) One of my favorite verses regarding transparency says that we are commanded to not only confess our sins to others, but also to pray for each other, as we see in James 5:16: "Therefore confess your sins to each other and pray for each other so that you may be healed. The prayer of a righteous person is powerful and effective."

> *Confession of sin is a must; it is not optional.*
> *"If we confess our sins, He is faithful and just and*
> *will forgive us our sins and purify us from*
> *all unrighteousness." (I John 1:9)*

We are also to pray for what God wants for us, not what we want. Knowing the scripture is how we know God's will, or what He "wills" for us. My prayers must always be to align my s with God's. And sometimes, my desires and prayers ᵢge because of His work in my life through prayer.

If we follow God's guidelines for prayer, we can know that he will answer them. James 4:2b-3 reminds us of this: "You do not have because you do not ask God. When you ask, you do not receive, because you ask with wrong motives, that you may spend what you get on your pleasures." Matthew 21:22 emphasizes that we are to "ask of God." "Whatever you ask in prayer, you will receive, if you have faith."

During my dark days, I prayed for God to take me home. I'm so grateful that He didn't. I had a family, but I didn't feel I was doing particularly good at rearing my children and tending to my husband. I was convinced that my family would be better off without me. Yet, God's will was for me to remain here. He has work for me to accomplish. One of my roles is to share with people how He has healed me for HIS glory.

Prayer isn't for us to get what we want from God. It is a privilege to communicate with Our Creator. God desires to hear our prayers! His word says they are like a sweet fragrance to Him.

Prayer isn't for us to get what we want from God.
It is a privilege to communicate with Our Creator.
God desires to hear our prayers! His word says
they are like a sweet fragrance to Him.

In Exodus, we read of the design and specific use of God's tabernacle. (It was a foreshadowing of Jesus and what would come.) In the tabernacle, in front of the thick curtain that blocked off the holy of holies where God was, stood a bowl of incense. The incense always was burned just before the pr̲i̲ entered the presence of God. The burning of this incense represented the prayers of the people.

When Jesus died on the cross on that dark and horrible day, the thick curtain in the Jerusalem temple was torn—dramatically ripped—from top to bottom. God tore that curtain to signify that we no longer needed priests to intercede for us. Now, because of the sacrifice of Jesus, we can boldly approach God Himself with our prayers!

The prayers of God's people are incense in heaven! "And when he had taken it, the four living creatures and the twenty-four elders fell down before the Lamb ... they were holding golden bowls full of incense, which are the prayers of God's people." (Revelation 5:8) In Old Testament worship, the aromas from the incense and the sight of the smoke were obvious and held deep meaning for God's people.

In early 2012, near the time that I had thoughts of being unworthy or not ready for the elders to anoint me, I felt convicted to fast and pray. God asked me to fast and pray on my niece's birthday—to pray specifically for her to conceive. She'd tried to have a baby for several years. (I later told her that I had prayed and fasted on her birthday. She replied that another friend had also prayed and fasted the same day. I was thrilled to know that we both were part of something God was doing.)

I decided to pray also for our son and his wife, who were trying to have a baby. Later, I learned that both sweet gals conceived near the time that God laid it on my heart to fast and pray. Yes, nine months later, their daughters were born a week apart. I'm grateful that I listened to and obeyed the Shepherd's voice to intercede in these situations.

My obedience in matters of confession, prayer, forgiveness, apologies, use of a head covering, church attendance, and many other things, were God's hand on my journey toward healing as he guided me through my two-year revival. He was preparing me to be ready to fully understand what He was about to do.

My church elders never did anoint me and pray for my healing. Before I could reschedule with them, God healed me. However, I believe that we all missed out on a tremendous blessing because I didn't follow through with the anointing.

This was just another time in my life as a Christian that I failed to do what I knew God wanted of me. We, the church, missed out on the blessing God could have heaped on top of the blessing He was already sending our way. Even though I failed in the flesh, I am encouraged that if I fail God, he is not changed by what I do or don't do. But, can you imagine how much more our church would have been blessed through my healing had they known that I was anointed and prayed over?

CHAPTER 15

YES, LORD, I BELIEVE!

When I reflect on the precious days that led to my healing, I'm amazed at how God was preparing me, this wretched woman, to bring Glory to Him.

My Bible study group in the fall of 2011 was studying *A Woman's Heart: God's Dwelling Place* by Beth Moore. As believers in Jesus, we have the Holy Spirit living in us. *We* are His dwelling place!

The study focused in the Book of Exodus, where we looked at the tabernacle, God's physical dwelling place built by the Israelites. However, we often reviewed other scripture to reinforce what we were gleaning from Exodus.

The study was designed so that group members studied individually using the workbook at home. When we convened as a group, we then watched Beth's video message related to the week's study. Now, when I review the answers that I recorded in my workbook that week leading to my healing, I'm in awe of my answers.

What I wrote in response to one of the lessons that week truly represented the work of God in my life. My own words jumped off the page. I was reminding myself that He is faithful even when I do not see His answers.

A question posed in the workbook was, "Have you ever recently questioned God's plan for your life and His timing?" I answered yes. The next question asked, "Has this study encouraged you to feel differently?" I answered no. In hindsight, I can't believe I wrote no. Maybe I just didn't understand the question in that moment. God surely *was working* on my behalf and *had been working* in my life up to that point. Maybe at the time of the study I just hadn't *seen* the difference in my life.

In hindsight, I can't believe I wrote no. Maybe I just didn't understand the question . . . God surely was working on my behalf and had been working in my life up to that point.

Another question in the workbook was "Can He make something good come from something bad? Read Romans 8:28: "And we know that in all things God works for the good of those who love him, who have been called according to his purpose." I wrote a resounding, capitalized YES as my answer.

Then we read Romans 8:29: "For those God foreknew He also predestined to be conformed to the image of His son, that He might be the first born among many brothers and sisters." The question asked, "What is His purpose?" I responded, "To conform us to the likeness of His son."

Then, I was posed with the question: "Will He Bless you?" And I was instructed to read Ephesians 1:3: "Praise be to the God and Father of our Lord Jesus Christ, who has blessed us in the heavenly realms with every spiritual blessing."

Yet, another question made me ponder. "Will He meet your needs?" The verse I read for that question was Philippians 4:19: "And my God will meet all your needs according to the riches of His glory in Christ Jesus." Yes!" I wrote, "according to His riches in Christ."

We are children of God, and therefore also co-heirs with Christ. We are royal priests because of our sonship. And priests are intercessors. This is the profound truth we read in Hebrews chapter 7 and Romans chapter 8. We see also in 1 Peter 2:9a this wonderful promise: "But you are a chosen people, a royal priesthood . . . "

It is incredible for me to review my journey with God those few days prior to my healing! God had beautifully orchestrated what I was studying while I was obediently fasting and praying. Through these lessons, I was reminded that God would make good come out of bad, He would meet my needs, and He would bless me with every spiritual blessing. I learned that I am of the royal priesthood, a co-heir with Christ, and an intercessor!

February 1, 2012, will always be burned on my memory as the day I heard from the Lord of the miraculous healing He'd planned for me.

February 1, 2012, will always be burned on my memory as the day I heard from the Lord of the miraculous healing He'd planned for me.

I had continued my fast into February 1. Overall, the day was incredible. I experienced great fellowship and worship with God.

That evening, Darryl was still away on business and I was home alone. I listened intently to a webinar. Leslie Vernick was speaking about whether God wants you to be happy.

After listening to Leslie's message, I sat, praying. Emotionally, I was healing from many years of listening to the lies of Satan. And relationally, our marriage had been a bit rocky for a time, though even that was healing.

Physically, I felt as if with God, I could handle this limited lifestyle that we had. And thrive in it.

Spiritually, I was closer to the Father than I'd ever been. I was content. Leslie's words had reminded me that God doesn't promise us happiness. Yet, I felt at that moment that I truly was happy. Sure, I still would have liked to not be suffering from RSD, but because God allowed it into my life, I would deal with it, with His help.

That's when I heard that still, small voice of my Savior gently say, "I am going to heal you." "What? Lord, is that really You?" I thought. But then, I knew. I knew without a doubt that it was true. God had just revealed to me that He would heal me.

God had chosen the perfect setting for that healing revelation. I was relaxing on the sofa in my wonderful Pittsburgh living room overlooking the woods. My ever-present companion, Spencer, was asleep next to me. The evening was more than serene.

I would have thought "God's going to heal me" if it were my own thought. But the thought that whispered through me that beautiful and calm evening was, "*I'm* going to heal you."

Imagine my poor husband when he called just an hour later! He is a believer and strongly believes in the power of prayer. However, to him it seemed to be out of nowhere that I excitedly shared that God told me He was going to heal me.

Beth Moore, acclaimed Bible study teacher and author of our study, may never know how God used the contents of her book and the specific order in which we studied those scriptures in His plan to change my life.

For me, in His divine timing, the study was ordered in such a way that I received confirmation the following day when I gathered with the study group. I knew then that it truly was the still, small voice of the Holy Spirit whispering in my soul that He would heal me.

> *I knew then that it truly was the still,*
> *small voice of the Holy Spirit whispering*
> *in my soul that He would heal me.*

The next morning, my Bible study group met—the same group of women who had anointed and prayed over me. Debbie, one of my closest friends in Pittsburgh, came to pick me up, even though she drove 25 minutes each way. She did this to be sure that I'd attend. She knew that very often I wouldn't be able to get myself out the door. Besides, driving was draining for me. Some mornings, she had to wait for me. But that morning I was up and ready.

I hopped in Debbie's car and told her what I had thought the Lord had whispered into my heart the night before. She was very encouraging in her enthusiasm. She was not at all skeptical; she had the faith to believe with me. Debbie had also been studying the same scriptures that week; thus, her heart was prepared to receive what I told her I'd heard from the Lord.

I chose to share with people right away that I believed the Lord. He'd told me that he was going to heal me. I was incredibly excited. I also knew that if I didn't say anything right away that I couldn't go back later and say, "Oh, by the way. God told me he was going to heal me." I'm sure my telling immediately was also prompted by the Holy Spirit. I took the risk to share because of my surety that I'd indeed heard the still, small voice of God.

I broadcast the news and found some people were skeptical. Even Christians were skeptical. Mostly, the Christians were skeptical. Those who don't know the Lord thought I was crazy. I remember one neighbor asking if I had "that disease" in the first place. Yes, indeed, I did.

> *I broadcast the news and found some people were skeptical. Even Christians were skeptical. Mostly, the Christians were skeptical. Those who don't know the Lord thought I was crazy.*

I might have been skeptical if someone had told me out of the blue that God was about to heal her. It's not something that happens all the time. In the past six months or so, I'd transformed from a prim and proper "church lady" into a hat-wearing, hand-raising, "amener" in church. It's no surprise that even my pastor was also a bit skeptical, as were my husband and most of my family members.

Many Christians doubt that God can miraculously heal someone. We are told to pray and He will answer. The skepticism anyone experienced was a result of me claiming that God *told me* He'd heal me. It was just that it seemed out of the blue for some people while I was on this spiritual high.

The lessons I was learning, along with the other sermon series, were instrumentally used by the Holy Spirit to push me into a closer walk through confession and obedience. All of this brought me to the place where I could *hear the voice of my Savior* and believe that healing would occur.

As Debbie, the others, and I listened to the video lesson, I was quite stoked about my promised healing. Beth spoke that day regarding Hebrews 7:15. "Wherefore He is able to also save them to the uttermost that come into God by him, seeing he ever liveth to make intercession for them."

I learned from the message that *dunamai*, the Greek word for able, means powerful. *Sozo*, the Greek word for save, means among other things, heal. The word *panteles* (uttermost or at all) means all completion.

When we came upon the word *uttermost,* Beth instructed us to turn to Luke 13:10-13 to see another use of the word *panteles*, this time translated "at all."

"On a Sabbath Jesus was teaching in one of the synagogues, and a woman was there who had been crippled by a spirit for eighteen years. She was bent over and could not straighten up at all. When Jesus saw her, he called her forward and said to her, 'Woman, you are set free from your infirmity.' Then he put his hands on her, and immediately she straightened up and praised God."

At that point, I focused on the eighteen years that the woman couldn't straighten up "at all." She was "unable," as the one translation of this Greek word states.

Eighteen years—the exact amount of time I was afflicted with RSD! This was no coincidence. I turned to Debbie and said, "I've had RSD for eighteen years!" It was one month less than eighteen years since I first was unable to hold a simple greeting card.

Debbie and I both had goosebumps realizing that we had just received confirmation that our gracious, loving, merciful, and wonderful Father had healing in store for me! I was unable to be healed from this affliction by medicine. God had promised that He was going to heal me.

Romans 8:17-18 reminds me of this truth: "Now if we are children, then we are heirs—heirs of God and co-heirs with Christ, if indeed we share in his sufferings in order that we may also share in his glory. I consider that our present sufferings are not worth comparing with the glory that will be revealed in us."

My deluge came upon me, a deluge of blessing. It was time—God's time. God came to me just as the spring rain described in Hosea. "Come, let us return to the Lord. He has torn us to pieces but he will heal us; he has injured us but he will bind up our wounds. After two days he will revive us; on the third day he will restore us, that we may live in his presence. Let us acknowledge the Lord; let us press on to acknowledge him. As surely as the sun rises, he will appear; he will come to us like the winter rains, like the spring rains that water the earth." (Hosea 6:1-3)

I felt my life now reflected these verses. God had promised to heal me, bind up my wounds, and revive and restore me so that I may live in His presence. He came to me as long-awaited rains, a deluge of blessing.

CHAPTER 16

FREEDOM FROM MEDICATION

I was in a season of fasting, praying, and intense Bible study. I had totally learned to believe in prayer and that God answers prayer. Intercessory prayer, and the other activities of my spiritual life that I described in Chapter 15, all led me to that one climactic evening.

God used the messages I was absorbing to prepare me to hear from Him. For reasons only He knows, God chose to heal me that special February day.

> *I was in a season of fasting, praying, and intense Bible study. God used the messages I was hearing to prepare me to hear from Him. For reasons only He knows, God chose to heal me that special February day.*

Romans 8:18 reminds us that our earthly sufferings will pale in comparison to the future glory that will be revealed when He comes again. "I consider that our present sufferings are not worth comparing with the glory that will be revealed in us." Isn't this a wonderful promise from our Heavenly Father who loves us more than we can imagine?

I experienced His magnificent glory when he healed me. The memories I have of the pain of RSD certainly pale in comparison. But even my earthly experience cannot be compared to the glory to come when I will be united with Him in Heaven for eternity.

If you are suffering in any way for Christ, please be reassured that your suffering won't compare to the glory you will experience one day.

My time of repentance and returning to God also resulted in a deluge of blessing, as we saw in Hosea 6:1-3. This passage reminds us that when we return to the Lord, He will come to us as the spring rains.

Those first few days, especially, and the few months after my healing, I felt as if I were being swept along in a rushing river of His blessing. The Sunday after I heard God's still, small voice, I was in the worship service at church. Darryl was still out of the country, so I was able to focus solely on the Lord.

That morning, I was overcome with praise for God. The content of the sermon and the song lyrics reminded me that I must now claim that my RSD was "in remission." I felt compelled to share with others that my healing was the Lord's doing.

God and God alone deserved the glory for my healing. I bounced up to our pastor as soon as the service ended and told him that I had to share that I was in remission. I was now healed! He didn't seem to know exactly how to respond to my exuberance. I could sense that he was a bit skeptical. Skepticism, as I've shared, was a response with which I became quite familiar.

I have often reflected on this time, pondering the blessing of my healing in the lives of my family and my friends. Yet, I truly know that my personal blessing of a closer walk with Him was the greatest of all.

There are rare occurrences of spontaneous remission from RSD. This fact may even be recorded in my medical records. I know without a doubt that my God reached down, touched me, and said, "Woman, you are healed from your infirmity."

I know without a doubt that my God reached down, touched me, and said, "Woman, you are healed from your infirmity."

I knew I'd never be able to wean myself off my medications without the confirmation I received from God. I'd suffered from a nasty illness, one with a level of pain rated higher than some cancers and even above amputation pain. Although, as high as my pain level was before all the medications, I don't believe mine was as intense as the pain other RSD patients suffer. My fear of getting totally free of medication was very intense.

After that first Sunday, I knew I no longer had RSD. It was time for me to stop my medications.

I'd run out of the Clonidine the week I heard God's still, small voice. I was not always good at re-filling my prescriptions in a timely manner. It was probably medically prudent at the time for me to continue the medication; however, I just never refilled the prescription. My body knew I was not getting the medication because my blood pressure was fluctuating.

I went to see my doctor the week after I heard that still, small voice, and, for the first of many times, I attempted to explain to a member of the medical community what I was now experiencing. Thankfully, he was a man of faith and believed me when I stated that God had healed me.

I . . . attempted to explain to a member of the medical community what I was now experiencing. Thankfully, he was a man of faith and believed me when I stated that God had healed me.

I was not feeling well from the lack of Clonidine, but my doctor decided that I did not need to go back on that pill. We then planned a strategy for me to withdraw from the Kadian. I would taper off slowly as my doctor prescribed. I wasn't addicted to the meds, but my body did depend on them. I now needed to wean myself off them. I didn't notice any withdrawal symptoms until the final week of the taper.

I endured an incredibly difficult and nasty, yet short, withdrawal from Kadian; however, it was indeed worth it. I couldn't wait to get it out of my body. I had carefully timed the taper so I'd still be taking Kadian while on a trip to Philadelphia to see our children.

Maybe I should not have started the taper until after our trip, but I was eager to get off medications. My body didn't require them anymore, and I was emotionally done with them.

Our family gathering was Sunday. By Saturday night, I was down to half a pill to take every other day. I thought I was doing so well that I didn't need the medication anymore. I assumed that it would be no big deal if I just skipped taking one half of a pill. What a poor assumption!

I just couldn't make myself take that pill that night. The next day, Sunday, was the day that I'd planned precisely not to experience any withdrawal symptoms. And yet, because of my not-so-smart decision the night before, I began experiencing signs of withdrawal by dinner time. I was starting to shake, feel sick to my stomach, became achy, and had an awful feeling all over. It was mild, but I still had trouble sleeping that night at my mom's. Even so, by Monday morning, as we prepared to return home, I still couldn't get myself to put one of the remaining pill halves in my mouth.

We drove five hours with me in complete withdrawal mode. The shaking, nausea, and a feeling similar to my skin "crawling" had become quite intense by the time we left mom's. It was a very long 5-hour drive, yet Darryl was kind and understanding. Maybe he wished that I'd taken the pill to help me endure the trip, though he never said so.

The following week was one I hope never to relive. My withdrawal from the Kadian continued. I was nauseated, shaking, and pacing. I remember lying in bed at night, earphones on, with a playlist of songs and just clinging to the comfort my Savior offered.

Many times throughout my illness, I'd lie in bed and the first words of a song would come to mind. I could only remember the first phrase, "Oh Lord, my God . . " I had no memory of the entire song nor its title; however, I knew the lyrics that I uttered brought me comfort.

I'd lie in bed and the first words of a song would come to mind. I could only remember the first phrase, "Oh Lord, my God . . . " I knew the lyrics that I uttered brought me comfort.

I lay there that week of my withdrawal, and many more after that, playing those same words through my mind repeatedly. I now remember the entire song, "How Great Thou Art." When we sing it in church, I am reminded of the comfort I got from that one phrase that repeatedly resonated in my mind.

Many weeks went by before I finally felt like myself again. My body needed time to recover.

I was already witnessing different changes in my body that signaled I'd truly been healed of RSD. One difference was that I could now hold hands with Darryl in church. When I suffered from RSD, we just couldn't hold hands. It simply hurt me too much.

I had greater strength, could walk the dog more easily, and bought a pair of sneakers. I hadn't been able to wear low-cut shoes since the pain had traveled to my legs. The backs of the shoes, touching the skin of my ankles, was just too painful. Instead, I wore clogs and boots, which touched higher up on my leg.

These new sneakers were so monumental to me that I posted a picture of them to social media. I was thanking the Lord daily for new things that I could now do, such as wear sneakers and babysit our granddaughter, Arden.

Sometimes, I'd thank God for an activity that I *didn't need to do* any longer such as riding a motorized grocery cart. Often, I'd take a picture of what I was thankful for and post it to social media. I'd post the words, "Because I can" and add the picture. I eventually coined a hashtag: #BecauseIcan.

My friends enjoyed these posts and thanked God along with me. I had so much for which to be grateful. To this day, I post things that I now can do—something I could not do before my healing. I Thessalonians 5: 18 reminds us that we are to "give thanks in all circumstances; for this is God's will for you in Christ Jesus."

The doctor and I agreed that I'd continue to take Cymbalta for a few months or even longer until my body had adjusted to the absence of the other medications. It didn't take me much more than a month or two before I refused to take that any longer. I just didn't need it—or want it in my system.

We decided too that I should return to aqua therapy to strengthen my muscles safely. This decision proved beneficial for me. I loved the warm pool water and my body gained strength from the exercise. My PT aide, Rachel, was a sweet girl from church whom I always enjoyed seeing.

I am, gratefully, a different person from whom I was before I was ill. I was a hyper go-getter, always busy "doing." Now, I have learned to relax and take things less seriously. In fact, I sometimes have trouble getting moving and knowing what to do next.

I have learned that I can entertain friends and family even if our house is not spotless. Before RSD, I was a hyper mess when I was expecting company. During my illness, I couldn't always do everything that needed to be accomplished for company or the holidays. I finally learned to worry less about preparations or the way the house looked. Over time, I realized that perfection in our home or the appearance of perfection in our lives is not the key to happiness. I can still enjoy our company or the holidays even if things are not perfect.

Perfection in our home or the appearance of perfection in our lives is not the key to happiness. I can still enjoy our company or the holidays even if things are not perfect.

Figuring out how to run my household again has been a work in progress. I'm now at a place where I enjoy my house being presentable, but perfection is no longer a mandate. This, I realized, is a good place for me to be, where I no longer place emphasis on my performance and try to be perfect in all regards. Now I care more about my guests than the condition of my home.

My new life of pain-free living was an incredibly exciting time, albeit complicated with the withdrawal and a sense of caution regarding what I could or should do as my body was recovering.

When the withdrawal period subsided, I was eager to push forward with strength in all areas of my life. I was busy as I attempted to find my place among the healthy.

CHAPTER 17

HEARING THE SAVIOR'S VOICE

I believe what I heard that day in February 2012 *was* the still, small voice of my Savior. I was not thinking about healing at that time. I was quite happy with my life and my relationship with God.

How did I know that what I heard was my Savior's voice? I knew because that wasn't the first time I'd heard His voice.

When we accept Jesus Christ as our Savior, the Bible says we are sealed with the promised comforter. This comforter is the Holy Spirit, the third person of the trinity. We worship God in one—God, the Father; God, the Son; and God, the Holy Spirit.

After His death and resurrection, Jesus was preparing His disciples for his return to heaven. He told them in John 14:16-17a: "And I will ask the Father, and he will give you another advocate (also translated as helper or counselor) to help you and be with you forever—the Spirit of truth."

Jesus promised his followers that even though he was leaving, they (and we) would not be alone. Other scripture tells us that the Holy Spirit comes to live in us. He helps, guides, strengthens, directs, and comforts us.

When we live in fellowship with God, we can learn to hear His voice. In John chapter 10, Jesus says sheep will follow only the voice of their shepherd. Sheep learn this because the shepherd spends time with them and takes care of them, just as a baby knows the sound of his mother's voice. When we spend time with the Lord through scripture reading, praying, and worshiping Him, we can sense when He's leading us. We recognize His voice.

I don't hear an audible voice of my Shepherd; however, I know that He prompts me or gives me thoughts that are not my own. Sometimes, these thoughts or words stand out as obviously from God's Holy Spirit. Other times, I sense a gentle "nudge," telling me that there's something I should be doing, such as something for another person. At other times, the thoughts I perceive are amazingly chilling in their clarity—it is indeed the voice of God's Holy Spirit speaking to my soul.

I've experienced several times when I heard the still, small voice of my Savior. These times never cease to amaze and delight me. This whisper sometimes comes when I *really* need to see the "handwriting on the wall." I wish to share two such occasions regarding our children.

> *I've experienced several times when I heard the still, small voice of my Savior. These times never cease to amaze and delight me. This whisper sometimes comes when I really need to see the "handwriting on the wall."*

On December 15, 1980, our older son, Eric, had reached four weeks of age. He was now at his actual due date. Someone who had a cold held him that day, and a few days later we knew he had caught a cold.

We followed typical protocol for an infant with a cold, but over that following weekend he got worse instead of better. By Monday evening, he was listless, lethargic, and wouldn't eat much. I called the doctor, but he thought I was an over-anxious, very young mom. I was only twenty-two. The doctor said to wait until the morning and call him again if Eric still seemed to be having trouble.

At 6 a.m., I arose with Darryl and we began our morning routine. I noticed that the baby was awake but not crying, so I picked him up to feed him. He nursed a bit, and then I laid him back in the bassinet to go back to sleep.

I sat on the bed and looked at my wee one. I saw that he was looking at me. This seemed strange; I'd never seen him do this. Then, I heard in my mind the words, "Mommy, pick me up."

I jumped to pick him up and he stopped breathing. I was panicked. In the neonatal unit, after he was born, he was quite lethargic as a result of his high bilirubin count. Nurses there taught us to jiggle him and flick the bottoms of his feet to get him to awaken. I immediately employed these methods, but I could not get him to breathe.

I ran with Eric, holding him tightly to my chest, into the bathroom where Darryl was getting ready for work. Darryl was and always has been my strength in situations such as this. While I was agitated, he calmly took the baby from me and we attempted to get Eric to breathe. Darryl even gave our precious son mouth-to-mouth resuscitation. He started breathing again. I immediately called the doctor who told us to bring Eric to the hospital emergency room.

We took our son to the emergency room, where we learned that he had pneumonia. The doctors assumed we had overreacted and had given Eric pneumonia as a result of the mouth-to-mouth attempt to revive him. Eric was admitted to the hospital. After he had stopped breathing several times that day and the next, medical personnel then realized that we hadn't overreacted. Our son was experiencing apnea spells. Eric remained in the hospital for more than a week.

As I reflect on that horrible day when we almost lost our precious infant, I see the Lord's hand at work. I believe it was a prompting from the Holy Spirit to pick up my son just before he stopped breathing. When Eric had looked at me from the bassinet and the thought "Mommy, pick me up" went through my mind, I knew I had to act.

I then made a call to my pediatrician's office. I had assumed that the office phone number was on a piece of paper lying on my nightstand. But, when we finally got back to our home that first night, leaving our five-week old alone in the hospital, I looked for the paper and could not find it. I don't believe it was ever there. I had just simply "remembered" the number—a number that I'd called just once previously. This was indeed another evidence of the Holy Spirit's work in our lives. It was my first time to "hear" my Shepherd's voice.

This was indeed other evidence of the Holy Spirit's work in our lives. It was my first time to "hear" my Shepherd's voice.

Near the fall of 1986, I went out to the front yard to play with my children and kick the soccer ball. I was not much into physical activity, but I did play with them regularly. That day, I wanted to make Graham run a long distance to get the ball. He had so much energy!

But, that day I was wearing shoes made of thin leather. When I pulled my leg back forcefully to swing hard to kick the ball, I hit the ground with the side of my foot. I didn't break my foot, but the pain worsened over time. I spent months on crutches. We found out that a bunion was causing my pain. I don't know if I previously had the bunion that I traumatized that day or if the trauma resulting from the impact resulted in the bunion.

Three months later, the doctor said I needed a bunionectomy, but it would be an entire year until I could schedule the surgery. It would have been a long year, except that I was walking through the living room one day when I heard the Shepherd's voice say, "Put the crutches in the corner." I realized that this was indeed my Shepherd's voice, so I stood the crutches in the corner.

At first, it still hurt quite a bit to walk without the crutches. But I soon learned from researching bunions that walking on the bunion would make it hurt, yet not walking on it also made it hurt. I had my first taste of walking the fine line of doing too much or too little.

In 2012, as I was withdrawing from the pain medications, the Lord allowed me to remember what He had whispered to me in 1994. He had said, "Healing is not what I have for you NOW." I had always remembered that He'd said, "Healing is not what I have for you." But I had dropped the "now" from the statement in my thoughts because I couldn't fathom that He may have healing in my future. I was a doubter.

I can't say that *He* allowed the lack of memory regarding the word "now," but I do believe it was for my best that I didn't think of it all those years. My finite belief was that I was to accept my RSD diagnosis and not fight to overcome it. It was just a part of my life, and I believed it to be something I'd live with for the rest of my life.

For eighteen years, I ignored that little word "now," only to remember it after He'd whispered His plans to heal me. He showed me that He planned to heal me all along; however, it would be in His timing.

> *For eighteen years, I ignored that little word*
> *"now," only to remember it after He'd whispered*
> *His plans to heal me. He showed me that He*
> *planned to heal me all along . . . .*

I may not have remembered that thought except that the following week, someone from church said to me, "Karen, we are praying for you. Why aren't you getting any better?" I knew the answer to that question because God had already said He wasn't going to heal me. I just knew deep down inside that the illness was something I'd have to endure.

When I reflect on the times when God "spoke" to my heart or mind, the thought seems profound! God's prompting in that moment was what I needed, and it reminded me that God was and is at work.

Near the time of a cancer diagnosis a few years later, I struggled in my prayer life and I was frustrated. The Holy Spirit whispered to my soul, "Be still and listen."

Near the time of a cancer diagnosis, . . . I struggled in my prayer life and I was frustrated. The Holy Spirit whispered to my soul, "Be still and listen."

For the next few months, I experienced that peace that passes all understanding. I now realize that Jesus was interceding for me. After my diagnosis of having cancer, I remember that He whispered to me, "I've got this," which reverberated through my soul. He had my life under His control.

It's difficult to explain these times when I know without a doubt that I hear directly from the Lord. I believe it's the work of the Holy Spirit teaching me, guiding me, and whispering to me. I know that I'm one of his "sheep" and He wants me to know His voice. John 10, verses 2 through 5 and 11 depict a beautiful story of the shepherd and his sheep: "The one who enters by the gate is the shepherd of the sheep. The gatekeeper opens the gate for him, and the sheep listen to his voice. He calls his own sheep by name and leads them out. When he has brought out all his own, he goes on ahead of them, and his sheep follow him because they know his voice. But they will never follow a stranger; in fact, they will run away from him because in fact, they will run away from him because they do not recognize a stranger's voice ... I (Jesus) am the good shepherd."

The events I've described are times I vividly remember that I heard the still, small voice of my Savior. Have there been others? Perhaps. But I am convinced that at these times I was being directed by the Lord. I was learning to listen to His voice so that when I heard, "I'm going to heal you," I knew for sure it was His voice. Besides, I never would have been willing to stop my medications without the knowledge that it was indeed His voice that was leading me.

CHAPTER 18

THOSE WHOM JESUS BLESSED WITH HEALING

Have you ever thought about the lives of those in scripture whom Jesus miraculously healed? Believe me, I have! I have experienced how difficult it is at times to acclimate to "normal" living since my healing. I haven't wanted to take my healing for granted, so I asked God what I was to do in response.

"What do I owe you, Lord?" was a mantra of mine for a long time. I finally realized that first and foremost, my responsibility was to give glory to God. Psalm 86:12 states: "I will praise you, Lord my God, with all my heart; I will glorify your name forever."

The verses God used to confirm that He was indeed going to heal me are found in Luke chapter 13. Verses 10-13 have tremendous meaning to me: "On a Sabbath Jesus was teaching in one of the synagogues, and a woman was there who had been crippled by a spirit for eighteen years. She was bent over and could not straighten up at all. When Jesus saw her, he called her forward and said to her, "Woman, you are set free from your infirmity." Then he put his hands on her, and immediately she straightened up and praised God."

The woman described in these verses was healed. She gave the glory to God, where it belonged. But just imagine, she couldn't straighten up for EIGHTEEN long—exceedingly long—years. What did her life look like after her healing?

Maybe she had a job that she could perform while she was bent over all those years. Perhaps she could now learn a new trade or skill. Maybe she had to learn how to fit into her family in her new, healed body. I wonder just how she adjusted to her healing.

I've also thought of the ten lepers whom Jesus healed. "Now on his way to Jerusalem, Jesus traveled along the border between Samaria and Galilee. As he was going into a village, ten men who had leprosy met him. They stood at a distance and called out in a loud voice, "Jesus, Master, have pity on us!" When he saw them, he said, "Go, show yourselves to the priests." And as they went, they were cleansed. One of them, when he saw he was healed, came back, praising God in a loud voice. He threw himself at Jesus' feet and thanked him—and he was a Samaritan. Jesus asked, "Were not all ten cleansed? Where are the other nine? Has no one returned to give praise to God except this foreigner?" Then he said to him, "Rise and go; your faith has made you well." (Luke 17:11-19)

Those ten lepers were forced to live outside the city where their families lived. They could not dwell among other people. They lived an extremely tough existence in pain and suffering. Then, suddenly, Jesus healed them. How well I understand that feeling!

Imagine returning to your home and telling everyone that you were healed. I wonder how the lepers were accepted back into their families and into society. Some people may have been skeptical and wondered who this Jesus was and how could He heal them. I remember how my family and friends reacted. They were skeptical, thrilled, and scared that I'd overdo it and cause the pain to return.

I would imagine that the lepers' families had grown accustomed to the lepers not being at home and probably had gone on living life without them. These now-former lepers had to find their places in their families. They had to find work. I'm sure there was much rejoicing that day, yet how did they return to "normalcy"? We just don't know.

We read in Matthew 8:8,13 of another miraculous healing: "The centurion replied, "Lord, I do not deserve to have you come under my roof. But just say the word, and my servant will be healed … Then Jesus said to the centurion, "Go! Let it be done just as you believed it would." And his servant was healed at that moment."

Jesus was certainly about the business of healing. "When evening came, many who were demon-possessed were brought to him, and he drove out the spirits with a word and healed all the sick." (Matthew 8:16)

Then we see the story of the woman with the issue of blood, as recorded in Matthew 9:20-21: "Just then a woman who had been subject to bleeding for twelve years came up behind him and touched the edge of his cloak. She said to herself, "If I only touch his cloak, I will be healed. Jesus turned and saw her. "Take heart, daughter," he said, "your faith has healed you."

Matthew 12:22 is yet another story of healing. "Then they brought him (Jesus) a demon-possessed man who was blind and mute, and Jesus healed him so that he could both talk and see."

In all these wonderful accounts, Jesus healed with just a word. Even just a simple plea for help grabbed the attention of our Lord. The common thread we see in these stories is that all these people showed faith in Jesus, the One who heals.

Not everyone who was healed rose up and praised Jesus. Have you ever pondered what their lives were like after they were healed? Do you believe all the thousands whom Jesus has healed went on to live perfect lives without any more pain, suffering, or hurt?

As awesome as their healings were, it was a mountaintop experience from which they eventually had to descend. They had to learn to live, in their healed bodies, among their families, their church families, and the townspeople.

I would imagine they all had habits and routines that had developed because of their afflictions or living conditions. They had become accustomed to their damaged bodies. Yet once they were healed, they still didn't possess perfect bodies. None of us have perfect bodies because we all live subject to the degrading effects of our sin-damaged world.

Though healed, they still cried, felt pain, had accidents, and suffered from allergies, cancer, arthritis, and numerous other ailments. Other people would disappoint them, get angry with them, be skeptical of their healing, and question if their healing had truly been of God.

All those precious ones whom Jesus healed also had to learn how to live with the knowledge that they encountered the Creator of the world in a way that few others ever had or would. I know some of what they may have gone through, because that same healing they received, I also received. Yet even in my healed state, I still had to get rid of many years of bad habits that I'd developed—some as a result of the RSD, others because of the many medications, and still others because I suffered from depression.

> *Yet, even in my healed state, I still had to get rid of many years of bad habits that I'd developed . . .*

I developed several interesting habits that took a long time for me to unlearn. For example, when my pain was at its zenith, I learned to let anyone around me do whatever they could for me. This saved me from increased pain and allowed me to do more of the things that I could easily do for myself.

I'd let others open doors for me, get things for me, and help me cook and clean. Because others did what they could for me, I was then able to do what others couldn't do for me, such as take showers, dress, and feed myself. For the most part, I could do those things, although I did require help occasionally.

One special memory I have when I needed help was during the first year I was ill, 1994. We wanted to celebrate our sixteenth wedding anniversary. Our tradition was to go away for a weekend. This was not realistic, however, because of my physical condition. So, Darryl found a beautiful way for us to celebrate. He hired a horse-drawn carriage to take us for a ride around the countryside north of Allentown.

After a beautiful ride, the carriage stopped at the restaurant where we had begun our journey. We had a lovely time while we waited for our dinner, and soon after the server brought us our meals, I went to the ladies' room. When I came back, my steak was nicely cut up for me. Darryl did this for me so that

I didn't have to sit there like a child while her parent cut her meat. What a thoughtful man!

After my healing, I had to learn not to ask someone else to please get me the milk or open a door or a jar. I was forced to relearn to automatically do everything for myself. After learning to do everything for myself, I then needed to relearn how to let people help me even if I didn't need help.

I was healed from RSD miraculously and completely, but I wasn't cured of my sinful nature. I'm sorry to say that is still with me. I am no longer chained by it, but it's still there, doing wrong. Paul expressed the ongoing struggle with the sin nature in Romans 7:18: "For I know that good itself does not dwell in me, that is, in my sinful nature. For I have the desire to do what is good, but I cannot carry it out." And verse 25 in the same chapter reminds us: "Thanks be to God, who delivers me through Jesus Christ our Lord! So then, I myself in my mind am a slave to God's law, but in my sinful nature a slave to the law of sin."

After God healed me, I faced, in those first few months, some significant challenges. First, I went through withdrawal from the medications my body no longer needed. Several months later, we prepared our house in Pittsburgh for sale. We moved and remodeled a house, then moved into it. I was busy doing what I thought was the Lord's work for me at that time—helping others. That is still my desire to be of help to others. I look forward to seeing how God will continue to use me.

One big question after my healing was whether I should return to work or remain at home. Working was challenging while I had RSD. I worked for a while during Ashley's college years, but it wasn't easy. I am blessed that I didn't need to continue to work during those difficult years.

God, however, gave me a job, and it was one I wanted. For several years after my dad's death, I'd dreamed of my mom coming to live with us. She finally did in 2017. I'm so very thankful that I hadn't pursued a job outside of my home because we only had two years with her before her death. I'm filled with gratitude that I had the blessed privilege to care for her.

Darryl and I also are blessed now to live close to his mother, Jean. She has lived alone since Darryl's dad passed away. It's an honor for us to be able to help her. I'm available to take her shopping, out to lunch, or to doctor appointments.

My desire is to remain flexible, being available to help others and volunteer where needed. Most recently, my "job" has been to record this memoir of my pain and suffering that led me to a revival with God. I don't know what God plans to do with my story of healing; I just know that I've recorded it in obedience to Him.

I don't know what God plans to do with my story of healing; I just know that I've recorded it in obedience to Him.

I've experienced a few health issues of which I know God could heal me; however, in His sovereignty, He has decided to let me suffer through these infirmities. I know that His timing in all matters is for my good, and ultimately for His Glory. I am more than willing to be used to glorify my God.

My pastor, Matt, and I were discussing verses that he and I each were individually memorizing at the time. He shared that he was studying Deuteronomy 6:4-9. I was curious as to what these verses contained, so, I read them, along with the rest of the chapter.

I read of God's charge to His people when they've been on the mountaintop with Him for a time. Then, they must return to live in the valley. It's not easy in the valley, but God gives us a plan and He is always with us.

"Hear, O Israel: The LORD our God, the LORD is one. Love the LORD your God with all your heart and with all your soul and with all your strength. These commandments that I give you today are to be on your hearts. Impress them on your children. Talk about them when you sit at home and when you walk along the road, when you lie down and when you get up. Tie them as symbols on your hands and bind them on your foreheads. Write them on the doorframes of your houses and on your gates." (Deuteronomy 6:4-9)

Later, in Deuteronomy 6, verses 23-25, we read: "But he brought us out from there to bring us in and give us the land he promised on oath to our ancestors. The LORD command-ed us to obey all these decrees and to fear the LORD our God, so that we might always prosper and be kept alive, as is the case today. And if we are careful to obey all this law before the LORD our God, as he has commanded us that will be our righteousness."

As I consider my new life after RSD, these verses also re-mind me that I must seek His kingdom first in all that I do.

CHAPTER 19

ENDURING YET
ANOTHER TRIAL

In the summer of 2014, two and a half years after I was set free from RSD, I began experiencing symptoms that I needed to discuss with my doctor. Over the next two months, I underwent tests, including a D&C and a biopsy in September.

My doctor spoke with my husband while I was in recovery. She believed that the successful procedure had probably "cured" me of my pre-cancerous symptoms. We were quite relieved, yet we needed to await biopsy results.

The Monday after my biopsy, the doctor requested an appointment for me to come in. The receptionist asked, "Can you come in this afternoon?" I replied a bit puzzled, "It hasn't been two weeks since the procedure. (I was told to make an appointment at the two-week mark.) I don't even have the results of my biopsy yet."

The receptionist continued. "I don't know about that, but the doctor would like to see you. Can you come in at 3:30?" At that moment, I realized that my results were probably back. I knew in my heart that what I'd learn wouldn't be good news.

My mind immediately went to the conclusion that I was, at the least, needing to have a hysterectomy.

The doctor had shared at our first office visit that, at the most, I may be pre-cancerous, which would require a hysterectomy. I don't know why she told me that because her information conflicted with the surgeon's. He said the reason a biopsy is necessary is that the condition *"could be"* cancer. In other words, a biopsy would confirm if a hysterectomy were needed.

Darryl joined me for the Monday afternoon visit to the doctor. She was pretty upfront at first, saying that I had cancer. Then she must have said two or three times, "Most women with this type of cancer . . . " I looked at her and said, "I take it I'm not 'most women,' am I?"

Apparently I suffered from uterine cancer, the easiest of all women's cancers to diagnose. It is also the easiest to treat, with very high success rates. However, these statistics reflect what the medical field labels as "grade 1" or "grade 2" cancers. Mine was a "grade 3," the most aggressive grade for my type of cancer.

Darryl and I had planned to go to the grocery store after I saw the doctor. When we left the doctor's office, I still wanted to shop for groceries. So, we went. I was probably in shock and just roamed the aisles, grabbing items, somewhat like a robot. With each item I picked up, the refrain, "I have cancer," played repeatedly in my head. I think I muttered it quite often as Darryl walked alongside me.

> *I was probably in shock and just roamed the aisles, grabbing items, somewhat like a robot. With each item I picked up, the refrain, "I have cancer," played repeatedly in my head.*

At first, I was numb. Here was yet another disease that I wanted to be healed from, but I wondered; "Why would God allow me to be victorious over cancer when He'd already healed me miraculously from the RSD?" I didn't believe I deserved another healing.

And then I remembered a prayer I had prayed about six months earlier. It was one of those prayers where His spirit leads us to say, "Whatever it takes, Lord." I had prayed this prayer for some loved ones. I turned them over to the Lord and said, "Whatever it takes, Lord, to bring my family to you."

I remembered that prayer, I was a bit excited in my spirit and thought, "This is it! This is what God is going to use to bring my family back to Him!"

This cancer diagnosis came in September 2014. Sometime during those days, I struggled with my prayer life. I just couldn't seem to verbalize any words to the Father. I remember again hearing that still, small voice whisper in my ear, "be still and listen." We are reminded of this in Psalm 46:10a: "Be still and know that I am God."

Then, I heard His still small voice again: "I've got this!" Darryl and I often felt we were truly living this wonderful promise from Philippians 4:7: "And the peace of God, which transcends all understanding, will guard your hearts and your minds in Christ Jesus."

I experienced total peace in the midst of the storm. My deepest desire during this time was that God be glorified through me and this trial.

I experienced total peace in the midst of the storm.
My deepest desire during this time was that God
would be glorified through me and this trial.

Before RSD, my greatest fear was to learn I had cancer. I was a bit of a hypochondriac when I was a child, especially since I was a huge fan of the television show, Marcus Welby, MD. I just knew that all those diagnoses I'd seen on that show were now what was wrong with me.

While suffering from RSD I'd say, "I'd rather have a cancer diagnosis than RSD." I felt this way because RSD was a day-after-day, month-after-month, year-after-year illness.

I knew no cure nor any dedicated treatments or medicines existed for RSD. Doctors use a combination of different drugs designed for various diseases and symptoms to treat RSD. It's a game of hit or miss to try to land on the right combination of medications for each patient. It was an unending future of pain, medicine and treatment. Once in a while, there's word of someone experiencing a spontaneous remission, but skepticism often reigns. Surely remission couldn't ever happen to anyone. Now, I didn't believe it could happen to me.

With cancer, on the other hand, one would most likely have surgery, chemotherapy, and or radiation and possibly be put into remission. I believed, therefore, that a cancer diagnosis would mean treatment that either worked or didn't work. In other words, I'd live or die. In my mind, dying and going to live with my Heavenly Father would have been my choice. Who wouldn't want to be relieved of constant pain and be instead in the presence of the One who loves her the most? I spent many days with RSD stuck in a dark place, begging the Lord to take me home. The fiery darts from Satan took me into those depths. Granted, as Christians we have promises from God's word as to how to combat Satan, but I didn't make use of them.

*Dying and going to live with my Heavenly Father
would have been my choice. Who wouldn't want to
be relieved of constant pain and be in the presence
of the One who loves her the most?*

My gynecologist, who presented me the cancer diagnosis, gave me the impression that I was in deep trouble with the advancement of the cancer. As we sat in her office, she tried to get in touch with the surgeon to whom she referred me, visibly frustrated at being unable to reach him. I once again was met with fear and wanted to have the surgery immediately.

I made the appointment with the surgeon in an unusual way, which gave me great encouragement. The "normal" routine for making an appointment with this doctor, the head of gynecological cancer at a nearby hospital, was for the referring doctor to fax the patient's records to his office. The surgeon would then read the patient's file and decide if he'd take the patient's case. When the surgeon made his decision, an office staffer called to schedule an appointment or to refer the patient elsewhere.

I didn't realize that they would call me back, so in a panic, I called the day after my records were sent. The receptionist checked with the doctor and said that the doctor wanted me to come in the following Monday. Then she realized that he wasn't available for a Monday appointment but that there was a cancellation for the next afternoon. I'd felt a strong need to see the surgeon because of the urgency my gynecologist had inferred.

I prayed that if I could see the doctor immediately, I'd believe that it was God's will that I go to this particular doctor. Otherwise, I knew of a cancer treatment center that I would try next. With such an immediate and positive answer to prayer, I felt comfortable with this doctor. It seemed God was directing my steps.

I prayed that if I could see the doctor immediately, I'd believe that it was God's will that I go to this particular doctor.

When I saw the surgeon, I was scheduled for a robotic-assisted total hysterectomy. Because the surgery was two weeks away, we could still take a much-needed business trip/vacation to New Mexico. We'd been looking forward to this trip. The timing of it was a tremendous blessing too.

I'd felt weak during this entire diagnosis phase and was getting more and more exhausted as the trip went on. But that did not stop me from enjoying the time with Darryl's co-workers and with my New Mexico family.

The surgery was a success and all the cancer was removed. The pathology report was quite encouraging. We felt the love of our family and were blessed by our church family during that time. Several people came to the hospital to pray with us, sit with Darryl while he waited, or to bring meals as I recovered.

It's interesting how medical professionals determine if a cancer patient needs chemotherapy, radiation, or both. Most, if not all oncology doctors use an equation to make this decision. The equation is based on what they find in the pathology report (I got the worst grade), your age (I fell into the "old" group), and the stage of the cancer (the best we could have expected).

I had a grade 3 stage 1a, which was determined at the time of the pathology report. If a patient has two of these three, it is recommended to undergo radiation. Therefore, the stage of my cancer saved me from chemotherapy.

The wisdom and urging of my daughter encouraged me to seek a second opinion regarding post-surgical treatment. Early on, I decided that if my family needed me to do anything as part of my recovery, I would try to accommodate them.

It was a huge deal to my children that I had cancer. My own mom was too old to endure seeing her daughter suffer with cancer. My poor family had already been through so much with me.

RSD had been very hard on my family and now we faced cancer together. Here it was only two years later that they were faced once again with the very real possibility of losing this new woman they were all still trying to get to know. I was clueless as to the pain they were enduring.

I fought the decision of whether to seek a second opinion, however. Because I felt that the Lord had directed me to the surgeon we used, I was apt just to say, "Okay. I'll go with his recommendation for radiation.".

Jan, the mother of our daughter-in-law, Anna, asked me to go to a concert during my recovery. It was a great afternoon. While talking during intermission, I mentioned that Ashley wanted me to get a second opinion on post-surgical treatment. But that I didn't know how to go about it.

God, in His Sovereignty, showed up. Jan "just so happened" to know the head of nursing in oncology at the cancer center I'd considered as an option. She was willing to put me in contact with this nursing director. The nursing director would then direct me as to how to go about getting a second opinion.

Through this contact, I got in to see a surgeon at the cancer center who studied my records and examined me. I went to that appointment praying that we'd get the same recommendation and that Ashley's mind would be put to ease. I, too, was looking for peace regarding the decision.

The Lord answered that prayer. The recommendation from my doctor was three rounds of radiation and this second opinion was the same. I felt the second opinion was a good thing because it gave me confidence that I needed radiation. It also put Ashley's mind at ease.

Another blessing was that this second gynecologist had been a colleague at one time of my radiologist. She said I would be in very good hands. I was so blessed to have him as my radiologist. He was comforting and gentle, which I really appreciated.

Some friends and family members were astonished that God would allow me to go through cancer after He'd healed me so miraculously. Some were angry, very angry. However, I can honestly say I was at a place where I was totally fine; enough so that Ashley noticed and told me I didn't have to be strong for the benefit of others. A close friend from my small Bible study group questioned whether I was really doing okay or if I was just "being strong."

I wasn't pretending to be strong; I truly was okay. Maybe onlookers wanted me to be a little more "not okay" so they'd know I was dealing with the pressure of the illness and just not stuffing it deep within me.

The scariest part of the entire experience occurred about a month after the surgery. I experienced some RSD-like symptoms. I was distraught and freaked out. How could I possibly freak out about this when God had healed me once from the RSD and had just allowed me to come through cancer successfully?

How could I possibly freak out about this when God had healed me once from the RSD and had just allowed me to come through cancer successfully?

I believe because I'm human I had to process my emotions mentally. I faced the firm idea that the RSD was returning as a result of the trauma associated with the cancer. I knew, too, that the reoccurrence of RSD could be a possibility and I'd discussed it with the anesthesiologist. However, I hadn't made an action plan with him if the RSD were to return. Finding a pain doctor proved to be too difficult in this situation. So, in a moment of rationalization, I decided to see my general practitioner.

Imagine my surprise and delight that the Lord had once again gone ahead of me and made a way! A year earlier, he'd directed me to a family doctor who understood RSD. He had other patients suffering from the syndrome. Also, his nurse had RSD as a teenager, so she was understanding. (Children are more likely to experience remission from RSD than adults.) The doctor recognized the symptoms I described as RSD and prescribed Cymbalta.

I believe the Lord knew when I chose a new family doctor after moving back to this area that I would need this exact doctor. Isn't our God wonderful? Matthew 5:8 states this reminder: "Do not be like them, for your Father knows what you need before you ask him."

I once again needed to arrive at a place where I finally said, "Okay, God. If this is what you have for me, I'll deal with it." I also knew that He would be with me in the worst of days and that I would know better *this time* to cling close to Him if indeed I were suffering again from RSD.

One of our pastors approached me and asked if I'd like the elders to anoint me with oil and pray for me. I joyfully replied, "Of course!" I, however, should have been the one asking them to pray for me instead of them coming to me. Yet, even in my misstep, the Lord healed me.

I have since endured several occasions when I suffered from pain. I feel as if each of those times, the pain was so intense that my sympathetic nerve system was ready to jump into overdrive. But, with prayer, prescribed medication, and trust in the Lord, I have been RSD-free since my healing that wonderful February many years ago. And now, I am cancer-free too.

I have been RSD-free since my healing that
wonderful February many years ago. And now,
I am cancer-free too.

I do not wish to minimize the trauma of having cancer. That is certainly not my intent. The experience was horrible and it really was a big deal that God brought me through it. I cried out to God in my RSD trial and in my cancer valley. He came through both times. He comes through whenever I remember to cling to Him and trust that "He's got this."

CHAPTER 20

MY LIFE AFTER RSD

It's a daily struggle to stay in close relationship with Jesus, isn't it? Our enemy, Satan, often sends distractions and untrue thoughts our way to keep our minds occupied with irrelevant and unimportant things. In Ephesians 6:16, the Apostle Paul calls these "fiery darts" (KJV) or "flaming arrows" (NIV).

I can just imagine: many small, but dangerous projectiles, any one of which can start a destructive fire. However, the Bible tells us in John 10:10 that "the thief does not come except to steal, and to kill, and to destroy. I (Jesus) have come that they may have life and that they may have it more abundantly."

When the Lord called me back to fellowship with him, I couldn't get enough of Him and His word. I was grateful that my daily schedule included time when I was alone in the house and had time to listen to sermons, read scripture, and pray. I suffered from insomnia, so I spent many nighttime hours listening to biblical messages.

I think of those many nights when I focused intently on podcasts. That was the perfect avenue for me; indeed, it was God's way to show me just how a believer should walk with the Lord.

I had immersed myself in the Lord. I felt as if He were calling me up a mountain, bit by bit, closer and closer to Him. I sensed at the time of my healing as if I were in His presence, standing on a mountaintop.

I felt as if He were calling me up a mountain, bit by bit, closer and closer to Him. I sensed at the time of my healing as if I were in His presence, standing on a mountaintop.

It was an incredibly heavy feeling in one regard; however, as I climbed that mountain, at one point I asked myself, "How can I possibly keep up this level of communing with the Lord?" It was all-consuming at times and a significant experience. As time progressed, I couldn't maintain such fellowship with God. I don't even believe that it's His design for us. We do have to be in this world, which means we are called to fellowship with others—both believers and non-believers—instead of just remaining on our mountaintop alone with Him.

Yet, it was during my time in His presence on the mountaintop that He healed me. I have found that I can't take that time nor that closeness with the Lord for granted. I believe God designs these mountaintop experiences for us. He doesn't mean for us to remain at such a high forever, and we cannot manufacture such times. There is no formula to follow for climbing to the top, just guidance in scripture to follow Jesus where he leads us.

I think of Moses and his mountaintop experiences. "The Lord descended to the top of Mount Sinai and called Moses to the top of the mountain. So Moses went up . . . Moses said to the Lord, 'The people cannot come up Mount Sinai, because you yourself warned us, 'Put limits around the mountain and set it apart as holy'." (Exodus 19:20, 23)

God *called* Moses to come up the mountain. There, Moses was in the very presence of the Lord. He descended from the mountaintop glowing because of his encounter! Can you just imagine Moses' countenance when he came off that mountain? It's a glow that said that he'd been in the very presence of God.

I felt like that for a while. I was flying high and glowing, experiencing the presence of the Lord. I had a glow about me—a glow that reminded me that God did something miraculous.

No one can craft a mountaintop experience on his or her own. Most of our lives we plug away, walking at times with God in the valley, seeking His kingdom, and awaiting His invitation to ascend the mountain again. Those mountaintop experiences sometimes accompany pain and suffering in our lives; however, standing in the presence of God is worth it.

I say that, yet while I had cancer, I didn't pray much. I considered it to be another season of just hanging out with Jesus, maybe this time in the valley of the shadow of death, and He was there holding my hand. I could feel Him but didn't have any words during that season. Despite a lack of words, I found that I had the "peace that passes all understanding," mentioned in Philippians 4:7.

During those times, I believe my Jesus was deep in conversation with the Father and actively involved in intercession on my behalf. After all, Romans 8:34 states this promise: "... Christ Jesus who died—more than that, who was raised to life—is at the right hand of God and is also interceding for us." What a wonderful promise! He takes time to intercede for us.

In April 2019, Pastor Matt Townsend, our pastor at Harvest Bible Chapel in King of Prussia, shared a sermon titled "Sifted." He explained that when we are being sifted as the chaff of wheat is sifted. This sifting process represents the tough times we go through. During those times, Jesus is at God's right hand praying to our Abba Father on our behalf! Jesus hurts and prays for us during those times. I'd never actually thought about Jesus praying for me during the hard times.

I stumbled ungracefully as I descended the mountaintop. I began to get involved in the busyness of life. I'm unaware of when I began slipping and allowing the things of this world get in the way of communion with the Lord. I wasn't sure how to live in this world again as a healed and well person. For all those years I had lived under a cloud of medications and physical limitations.

> *I stumbled ungracefully as I descended the mountaintop. I began to get involved in the busyness of life.*

I believe that sometimes my prayers aren't going to change the course of my life; rather, they are designed to help me stay aligned with His will and to trust Him. Either way, I am grateful for His work in my life.

There's a peace that comes when I put even the little things into His hands. When things work out the way I need or want, I feel as if He has answered my prayer. But would it have turned out that way anyway? Maybe so or maybe not; but I've rested in Him and know that all will be well either way.

I've also witnessed some interesting answers to prayer. I've prayed in the past over such things as a parking spot. Did

God choose to open a good parking spot just for me? I like to think so because I know He cares about the little things in my life. I praise Him that I got the parking spot I requested.

I saw an answer to prayer once that really, in the grand scheme of things, probably didn't matter. I believed that God was wanting to orchestrate a trip for me—to tag along on a business trip with Darryl. His sister, Crystal, and I were praying that I could find someone to watch our dog so I could accompany Darryl to New England. If I could locate a dog sitter and go along, then, I could fellowship with family.

However, the Thursday before we were to leave, I had no one to watch the dog. I asked myself, "Does God really care if I find someone to watch my dog?" Yes, I believed so because I was convinced that God wanted me to make this trip.

Maybe Darryl's sister and I just needed time together, or maybe I was going to meet someone with whom I would share my story. Or maybe my husband and I really needed this time away. All I know is that after praying about it and leaving it in the Lord's hands, I was able to relax. I searched online and found a company that connects pet owners with "pet hosts." I found someone just a few miles from my home who could watch our dog in her home. My prayer was answered, and my problem was solved. We had a great trip and a wonderful visit with Darryl's sister.

When God answers prayers such as this that we deem small or insignificant, we must be reminded of the verses that tell us how much He cares for us.

When God answers prayers such as this that we deem small or insignificant, we must be reminded of the verses that tell us how much He cares for us.

Matthew 6:25-27 records this truth from Jesus: "Therefore I tell you, do not worry about your life, what you will eat or drink; or about your body, what you will wear. Is not life more than food, and the body more than clothes? Look at the birds of the air, they do not sow or reap or store away in barns, and yet your heavenly Father feeds them. Are you not much more valuable than they? Can any one of you by worrying add a single hour to your life?"

Because Peter knew this teaching of Jesus (1 Peter 5:7), he tells us to "cast all your anxiety on Him because He cares for you.

I have some specific prayer requests that I've chosen not to nag God about. I'm trusting Him in these situations. However, I've also learned over these many years of pain and heartache that I need to pray about these things occasionally.

I find sometimes that I pray about something and then don't think about it for a long time. Then, when I remember, I need to talk with the Lord and say, "Yep! I remember that one too!" It's certainly not the time to stress over it. Obviously, the God of the universe can handle my requests!

I have a specific request that I placed in the Lord's hands long before the RSD came into our lives. He once reminded me of this request. I was just on the verge of agitation mode when He reminded me to trust Him. It had been many years since I'd first prayed that prayer and a long time since I'd remembered. When I did remember who was in control of the situation, it made all the difference to me. I was able to rest in Him, accept things the way they were, and wait for His timing. How particularly important it is to take all our requests to the throne of grace and leave them there.

Other times, however, I worry that I'm not caring enough nor consistent enough to keep praying repeatedly. In those times, I'm reminded that God does not want us to be dripping faucets.

I must also realize when the Lord reminds me about certain requests that He is reminding me of this: He's not forgotten, and neither should I.

During those RSD years, I suffered many dark days of pain and mental anguish. I didn't turn to the Lord. I wallowed. I tended to want to use the excuse that it was the medications that caused my negativity, but I really think it was my spiritual state that led me into those dark moments. I'm quite sure, too, that my family didn't realize my mental state of despair.

My wallowing came through in the emotions of bitterness, anger, and being overwhelmed by circumstances. I wasn't praying about these things and resting in the comfort of knowing that my Savior was interceding on my behalf. Because I didn't trust Him, the pain was more difficult to deal with at times, which made me more miserable. I wasted many years not praying, seeking, and trusting God.

Even when we are not obedient to Him, God can work through us. When we are obedient, the Lord showers us with blessings beyond belief.

My physical change has resulted in significant adjustments. In the spring of 1995, about a year after I first went to Kutztown for physical therapy, I was walking on a treadmill. I could only walk for one minute before exhaustion overtook me. I don't recall achieving more than five minutes on the treadmill each time I went for therapy. Just to think that this was when the RSD was only affecting my hands and arms. My legs were not yet an issue.

I gradually increased my ability to walk. I was fine if I didn't swing my arms too much, causing my shoulders to hurt. I often used a sling to stabilize my shoulder and wrist. We had moved close to Eva, a cousin, in 1995. I had the strength to take walks with her for a season before the RSD jumped to my legs. I loved those walks with Eva, who was more of a sister to me than a cousin.

When the spring of 2011 arrived, I was ready to try hiking a trail. I had significantly improved from the Kadian and Cymbalta, now a part of my daily meds routine. My hips had healed and chiropractic care for my back was working great. I'd been walking Spencer at a park where there was a short path around a small lake. I was getting stronger.

Darryl passed a lovely wooded trail each day on his way to work in the outskirts of Pittsburgh. We dreamed of being able to walk along that trail together. That spring, we took a drive past the Trillium Trail and were astonished at the beautiful white trillium blossoms. But I really wanted to view them up close.

With careful planning, we found out that from one entry point along the road to the next was only one-fourth of a mile. This was doable.

We chose a beautiful day, parked the car, and took our hike. I waited while Darryl went back for the car and came to pick me up. I was exhausted, but happy to walk that trail.

Just recently, we hiked into an 800-foot gorge and out again. My lungs protested but my body did not. I had no pain. God has been so good to me with the things He has allowed me to experience again. Hiking the gorge was a wonderful, new experience.

During those years of RSD, I was always amazed at people who could walk a mile, or even several at one time. My mind had a hard time realizing just how limited I was in what I could do and how weak I was. Now, I sometimes walk three miles at a stretch. I still seem to be limited, and since having cancer, I'm finding I still tire out and need a crash day after several days of physical activity. I have found now that I can push myself. I don't have to limit what I want to try for fear of how I'll feel afterward.

After God healed me, I wanted to do everything I hadn't done for those many years. I was wearing out my husband with my requests! He had to gently remind me that we both had aged eighteen years during my illness.

Life after RSD has been exciting, exhausting, challenging, and fraught with struggles that I cannot even begin to share. God has been here with us through it all. He had a purpose for my healing.

> *Life after RSD has been exciting, exhausting, challenging, and fraught with struggles that I cannot even begin to share. God has been there with us through it all. He had a purpose for my healing.*

I am not special because God healed me nor was it because I am special. He *chose* me to heal, yet I can't explain why. My life since has been anything but perfect. So, why did He heal me? Why had I suffered so much and then been blessed with healing? I can't answer that question. I believe in my heart that God healed me for His glory.

I came down from the mountain after my healing. I experienced a new life—physically, emotionally, and spiritually. I'm enjoying the times I can be with my family, whenever and for however long we want, without knowing I will suffer from pain as a result. I can be the grandmother I always wanted to be. I can now be involved in my family's daily life, holding sleepovers for the grandchildren, and enjoying my crafting again. I want to be a joy-filled wife, mother, and grandmother who dotes on her family.

Darryl and I have found that we enjoy our life together now, although I am sure it looks different because of the RSD. We will never know what we'd be doing now if not for those eighteen years. I know this however: I'd not go back and change any of what we experienced. We know our experiences formed us into who we are now. The pain we endured was worth it. Now, God uses our lives to bring glory to Himself.

I rediscovered that earnestly praying to God and trusting in Him helped give me the right perspective on all these new adventures. Despite the ups and downs of my life, I appreciate His sovereignty and rejoice in His blessings.

As I was growing up in church, we often sang "The Doxology." In my gratitude to God at this stage of my life, that beautiful stanza written in 1674 seems quite fitting:

> "Praise God, from whom all blessings flow;
> Praise Him, all creatures here below;
> Praise Him above, ye heav'nly hosts;
> Praise Father, Son, and Holy Ghost.
> Amen."

CHAPTER 21

WHY NOT ME?

Have you ever heard of "survivor guilt"? *Medical News Today* defines survivor guilt as "when a person has feelings of guilt because he or she survived a life-threatening situation when others did not. It is a common reaction to traumatic events . . . ."

An Internet search of "survivor guilt 9/11 (2001)" results in numerous articles and commentaries. Survivors of this horrendous event still, to this day, feel guilty for having survived when others did not.

I can honestly say that I've struggled with feeling guilty that God chose to heal me. I call this "healed guilt." Satan has attempted to distract me with questions such as "Why me?" or "What did I do to deserve His great blessing?" or "What do I owe Him for it?"

I've even been afraid at times to share my story with people. I'm fearful that my healing would cause jealousy or hurt because God healed me and not them, or, more importantly, their loved one.

*I've even been afraid at times to share my story
with people. I'm fearful that my healing would
cause jealousy or hurt because God healed me and
not them, or, more importantly, their loved one.*

When I was first ill with RSD in 1994, I struggled with thoughts of "Why me?" I whined and moaned about my circumstance. Darryl replied that if my illness were what God intended for us, we would just deal with it. I accepted both his words and my status; we would manage to cope somehow.

So, I learned, with practice, to change my "Why me?" to "Why *not* me?" There is no reason for anyone not to be the sick one, the hurt one, or the disappointed one. We live in a sin-filled world, where degradation is a given.

Romans 8:21 clearly states: "That the creation itself will be liberated from its bondage to decay and brought into the freedom and glory of the children of God." This verse declares the entire creation has been groaning with pain. Much like a mother in childbirth, right up to this time in history.

All of creation has been affected by the original sin that was brought into the world. At the beginning of time, in the garden that God purposed for eternal life, Adam and Eve believed the lies of Satan.

As an extremely sick person, I endured numerous attacks of the enemy. Satan seemed to take great pleasure in making me believe I was not worthy of love from my family, friends, or even God.

Satan also sent his fiery darts to distract me as I was penning this memoir. He taunted me with, "Why were you the one whom God healed?" He also asked, "Why isn't this person or that person being healed?" And finally, he was rude enough to whisper to me, "You shouldn't tell people you about your healing because they may be angry that their loved one wasn't miraculously healed."

> *Satan also sent his fiery darts to distract me as I was penning this memoir. He taunted me with, "Why were you the one whom God healed?"*

I've learned, however, to change my mantra to one that is pleasing to God! My "Why heal me?" is now, "Why *not* heal me?" God is holy, righteous, and sovereign. If He chooses to heal one person and not another, it is His Sovereign right. I was not any more deserving of a miracle than the next person. I believe God chose me for his own reasons and according to His plan.

If God can use *me* to glorify Himself, then why *not* me?

So often we believe that our struggles are unfair. We ask God, "What did I do to deserve this?" Well, let's be truthful! What have we ever done to deserve not to have problems?

Some people believe the world owes them—happiness, wealth, popularity, and other life dreams. God never promises us any of these things. He promises us peace, love, and joy which come from trusting that He knows what's best for us. Sometimes this means discipline, pain, and suffering. He's a good, good father who always provides what we need.

Scripture is chock full of stories of people who were in trouble because of their own failings, including many stories about the Israelites, God's chosen children. They often lived in disobedience. As a result, God allowed or caused something difficult in their lives to discipline them and drive them back to Himself. Other times, circumstances arose that brought suffering— suffering that wasn't a result of one person's wrongdoing.

Let's consider King David as an example. Basically, he lusted after Bathsheba and raped her. (Just imagine if she tried to say "no" to the King of the land.) David's sin caused the death of two innocent people and left a wife and mother in grief. Bathsheba's husband and baby were innocent; yet they bore the consequences of David's sin. The pain Bathsheba suffered was not her own doing, but she suffered greatly the loss of both her husband and her baby.

At other times, God even uses us when we are living a life of sin, as was the case with Rahab, a prostitute in the city of Jericho. Rahab hosted the two Israelite spies and lied to protect them. It's fascinating to see how God used her *even through a lie!* And isn't it interesting that Rahab is included in the "Hall of Faith" in Hebrews chapter 11 where the writer acknowledges her great faith.

I wonder how much more God would have been glorified if Rahab had not lied. What if she just had allowed God to protect the spies with His power?

I wonder how much more God would have been glorified if Rahab had not lied. What if she just had allowed God to protect the spies with His power?

I must be careful not to sin even when I believe it will help Him. I've learned from this story that I won't thwart God's plans with my disobedience; however, God's power is shown more clearly when we allow Him to work in our obedience.

Do we ever want to believe that it really could be God who allowed or caused hardship in our lives? Would God ever do this purposely?

I believe that God allows and "prescribes" difficulties in our lives. He only allows circumstances that will be for our good and His Glory. I'm convinced that my time of suffering from RSD was one of these "prescribed" circumstances.

When we finally accept that He is in charge and say, "Whatever Your will, Lord," we can live our lives much more peacefully and with the right perspective. I've learned that perspective is so important.

How often do we ignore the truth that our sin could well be the reason we hurt and suffer? I've been there. It took me a long time to come to terms with my sin and confess it, only to be revived by my great and wonderful Heavenly Father. Through this lesson, I learned that nothing in my life "just happens." Everything in our lives is designed to bring God glory!

I can fight the sufferings, events, or situations that God allows, or I can seek His face and His comfort. In doing so, I can wait patiently for that perfect timing when He will be glorified through me.

Can you fathom the honor we have to bring Glory to God, the Creator of the world? It's amazing that God would use woefully sinful, wretched humans to bring Glory to Himself!

I believe we have trouble either because of our sin, our twisted, fallen world, or God's design. When we have a hardship come upon us, we must ask, "Why is this happening, Lord?" Our intent must be to trust Him and to ask Him to reveal to us if we are responsible for our own hardship.

Could it be that we harbor unconfessed sin? Could it be that we stepped out of His will and have not sought His face nor His forgiveness?

When we are faced with disease, hurt, or trials, we should always draw near to God and seek Him. As the psalmist says in Psalm 46:1, "God is our refuge and strength, an ever-present help in trouble."

When we are in the place of our refuge, safely tucked under his wings, that's when we must talk with Him. This safe place is where we ask Him to reveal to us what we must learn or do in our situation. Psalms 91:4 reminds us: "He will cover you with His feathers, and under His wings you will find refuge; his faithfulness will be your shield and rampart." God always wants to hear from us.

The good news is that repenting and turning to God, or turning back to God, is always in His timing. He allowed me to flounder in my walk with Him for sixteen years before I finally listened. When I truly listened, I heard Him call me back into fellowship with Him.

God also granted me the repentance I needed at the time He wanted me to repent. All the events leading up to my healing represented pieces of a vast puzzle, all being perfectly put into place. He wanted to use my healing for His Glory. This verse, 2 Timothy 2:25, states that it is God who grants repentance: "Opponents must be gently instructed, in the hope that God will grant them repentance leading them to a knowledge of the truth."

I sincerely believe His healing for me was in His perfect timing. God knew that February 1, 2012, would be the date He would speak to me and heal me.

My prayer for you, dear reader, is that God would grant you the repentance you need in your life and lead you to a knowledge of the truth, just as this verse promises. God desires that all of us draw close to Him. He designed us all with a void in our hearts—a void that only He can fill.

God desires that all of us draw close to Him. He designed us all with a void in our hearts—a void that only He can fill.

I did not deserve the healing God allowed in my life. It's not about me. It's all about God. My health. My happiness. My trials. My hurts. It's all about Him and what brings Him Glory.

I am bound for Glory. Someday, Jesus will call my name and I will go home to Him. What a magnificent day that will be! It will be sad for those I leave behind, but I will be in the best place ever for me—a place that He has promised for those who put their trust and faith in Him and Him alone.

For now, God has preserved my life and raised me from the pit! I cried out to my Father in heaven as the psalmist wrote in Psalm 30:2, "Lord my God, I called to you for help, and you healed me."

I had cried out to Him for the healing of my dry, cracked soul, which was littered with the weeds of sin. In that horrible state, I was unable to experience the joy of my salvation.

Picture me, standing on a mountaintop, exclaiming that God, the one true Lord, healed me! He healed that dry soul, teaching me many biblical truths along the way, and gave me greater joy than I'd ever had to that point. Then, He chose to heal me physically. I can't possibly repay God for the miracle of physical healing he bestowed upon me.

...ı certainly praise His holy name and give Him all ıne Glory!

Sometimes we wait, as I did, a long time to see God working in our lives. However, He desires that we learn to live lives that honor and glorify Him while we wait to see what He's doing. It's not our role to ask, "Why me?" We should ask, rather, "Why *not* me, Lord?"

> *Sometimes we wait a long time to see God working in our lives. However, He desires that we learn to live lives that honor and glorify Him while we wait . . .*

My life should bring Glory to Him, yet I sadly miss that mark way too often. Even after having a most glorious experience with my Lord and Savior, I still fall. Just because I have felt the very touch of God on my life doesn't mean that I am a perfect example of a Christian. I, just as the Israelites, still flounder and fail. The good news is that I (we) serve the God of second chances!

This wonderful passage in Lamentations 3:19-26 is indeed my testimony: "I remember my affliction and my wandering, the bitterness and the gall. I well remember them, and my soul is downcast within me. Yet this I call to mind and therefore I have hope: Because of the Lord's great love we are not consumed, for his compassions never fail. They are new every morning; great is your faithfulness. I say to myself, 'The Lord is my portion; therefore, I will wait for him.' The Lord is good to those whose hope is in him, to the one who seeks him; it is good to wait quietly for the salvation of the Lord."

EPILOGUE

A s I was compiling my thoughts for this book, before, during, and since my healing, I never could have imagined what was still to come.

Within a year of my healing, we had a new grandchild, a new home, a new church family, and Darryl had a new job. I was certainly counting my blessings.

Within a year of my healing, we had a new grandchild, a new home, a new church family, and Darryl had a new job. I was certainly counting my blessings.

There were still some hard times to come, especially during my fight with cancer. However, we experienced some great highs in addition to the new grandchild, such as our daughter's wedding, some special vacations, and many other blessings. I was enjoying my new life free of RSD.

Six years after my healing, we began a very painful journey. It started with a heartbreaking chain of events in the life of our son, Graham, and ended with his death in December 2018. Losing a child is excruciatingly painful. This pain was by far the most difficult we've ever experienced.

I can't end this book without sharing about Graham. He was such a vibrant part of our family. Since the time he was an infant, he was fun-loving and full of personality. He was always the life of the party, sharing stories, jokes, and witty comments.

Graham was fearless, too, often to his detriment. He was intensely loyal and cared deeply for people, not just friends and family. Graham was a helper. After he died, a friend described him in an emotional post as "Graham, the human tender." I suppose that was his calling—to be a kind touch to humankind. In his absence, we have huge holes in our hearts. We all loved him so very much.

Graham spent the summer before his death in Virginia. Much of that time he was reading an early draft of the manuscript of this book. He read it, approved it, and encouraged me to complete my work. He truly motivated me to share my story. He was always a great cheerleader for me in whatever I attempted.

> *Graham . . . read it, approved it, and encouraged me to complete my work. He truly motivated me to write and share my story. He was always a great cheerleader . . .*

That summer, Graham wrote a sweet letter to his father and me. His words echo in my heart and encourage me to this day: "I more enjoy the fact that you *can* actually be going to something like a race (we had gone to a NASCAR race, something I never could have done with RSD), especially after reading Mom's book and remembering what a miracle it is to have a *healed* mom!!!!!!! Just writing to let you know how much that, and strength I have pulled from that, mean right now! (And always will)" Little did he know that I would be forever be encouraged from those precious words.

We'll never know what was really going on inside of Graham that made him take his own life. I could tell you about the awful things he had been through—things that resulted in discouragement and depression. I could share about his struggles that he was good at hiding.

Graham was living with us at the time of his death, but we honestly never saw it coming. We thought that after he'd endured a horrific year, he was choosing to rebuild his life. It seemed on the surface that he was trying his best, putting the pieces back in place one by one. However, life was still quite difficult for him. Darryl tried to encourage Graham by saying that his life was in a "rebuilding phase," slowly adding one brick at a time, as the story of Nehemiah in the Bible.

We said goodbye to Graham December 15, 2018. But we know we'll see him again someday.

We also lost Darryl's dad and my mom during this time of heartache and grief. Darryl's dad died ten months before Graham; Mom died just a month after. Graham's funeral was hard enough, but then we found ourselves back at the same cemetery, next to Graham's fresh gravesite, to bury my mom, just thirty-three days later. It was almost too much to bear. I lost it.

As difficult as it was to lose these family members, we clung to Jesus, found our refuge in Him, and trusted what He was and is doing. While we were still grieving deeply, mostly ham, but also over my Mom and Darryl's dad, we received glorious news. Ashley was expecting her first baby. We were elated! This was God's good gift to our entire family, not just a blessing for Ashley and Nate.

However, after a few months, we received devastating news; the baby would not survive after birth. Wham. What a blow! Three months later, we said goodbye to our precious little Ruby Jean. She lived just 34 minutes in this world. This was yet another excruciating loss, which was so difficult for all of us.

I cried out to God in the midst of my pain when I had RSD. I cried out to God in the midst of my pain when I lost my son. I cried out again over the loss of baby Ruby. These losses made no sense at the time; but God was there. His Holy Spirit provided comfort. We also gained perspective from His word; the support of friends and family; and in the end, we found peace. God is good all the time. His mercies are new every morning.

> *...God was there. His Holy Spirit provided comfort.*
> *We also gained perspective from His word; the*
> *support of friends and family; and in the end,*
> *peace.*

My husband often reminds people that Jesus said these beautiful words, as recorded in John 16:33: "I have told you these things, so that in me you may have peace. *In this world you will have trouble* (italics added). But take heart! I have overcome the world."

Yes, this passage is indeed true. I've lived it. God continues to amaze me. I've shared what I learned through my RSD journey. I hope one day to write the lessons I learned from the loss of my son.

We miss our precious Graham. We are thankful that according to the promises of God, and because Graham had trusted in Christ's death on the cross for his eternal salvation, we will see Graham again one day in heaven! How wonderful that we have this blessed assurance.

Friend do not give up! Be hopeful! Our God reigns. He has a purpose and a plan for everything you are going through. I pray that you learn, as I did, to trust Him. He is a God of purpose. After all, He took me, hand in hand, on my journey from pain to purpose. He will do the same for you.

I've come to greatly appreciate the song *All Things New* by the Christian group, Big Daddy Weave. Darryl and I went to one of the group's concerts just before the COVID-19 pandemic hit Pennsylvania in 2020. In the midst of heartache such as ours with my physical pain for eighteen years and losing our son, we pressed into God—our God of mercy and love who makes all things new!

All Things New

I've heard You can take what's broken and make it whole again
Well, here's the pieces of my heart, what can You do with them?
'Cause I can't hold them all together anymore
So I let them fall surrendered to the floor

You make all things new
You make all things new
God of mercy and love
Do what only You can do and make all things new

Only You can bring such beauty from the depths of all my pain
Only You can take this shattered heart and make it beat again
Oh, You hold us all together in Your hands
I surrender all I have and all I am

You make all things new
You make all things new
God of mercy and love
Do what only You can do and make all things new

APPENDIX

My dear reader,

Thank you for reading the story of God's amazing touch on my life.

The most important message you can take away from my book is that God is real and loves you just as much as He loves me. I believe my sin has been forgiven because I have accepted Jesus' death on the cross as payment for my sin. Because of this, I am no longer separated from God.

I have no doubts that I will spend eternity with Him in heaven instead of in hell. Hell is a very real place where sinners will be separated from God in complete darkness and live in burning anguish. The Bible makes this very clear.

You, too, can know that you will go to heaven one day. I'm writing this in 2020, in the midst of the COVID-19 pandemic when our mortality seems to be staring many of us in the face.

If you are ready to accept Jesus Christ as your Savior, it's as simple as ABC:

> *Admit* you are a sinner and have made mistakes. "For all have sinned and fall short of God." (Romans 3:23)

> *Believe* that Jesus is God's son, died on the Cross for you, and rose from the grave on the third day. "For God so loved the world that he gave his one and only Son,

that whoever believes in him shall not perish but have eternal life." (John 3:16)

> *Confess* Jesus as Lord of your life. Romans 10:9 and 10 state "that if you declare (confess) with your mouth, 'Jesus is Lord,' and believe in your heart that God raised Him from the dead, you will be saved."

For it is with your heart that you believe and are justified, and it is with your mouth that you profess your faith and are saved. Seek to follow Jesus. You can learn how by reading the Bible, praying (talking to God) and finding a good church to attend.

If you have done this, tell someone! I'd love to hear of your decision to follow Christ!

Love,

Karen

healedforhisglory@gmail.com

For more information regarding salvation and how to get to heaven, check out:
www.gotquestions.org/Romans-road-salvation.html

RECOMMENDED RESOURCES

RSD Information
For a description of RSD and the McGill Pain Index, see rsds.org.

Reading Resources
Miller, Paul. *A Praying Life: Connecting with God in a Distracting World.* Navpress, 2009

Moore, Beth. *A Woman's Heart: God's Dwelling Place.* LifeWay Press, 2007

Gregory, Susan. *The Daniel Fast: Feed Your Soul, Strengthen Your Spirit, and Renew Your Body.* Tyndale, 2010

Vernick, Leslie. *The Emotionally Destructive Relationship: Seeing It, Stopping It, Surviving It.* Harvest House Publisher, 2007

Nichols, Natalie. "America's Founders & President: Proclamations for Fasting and Prayer." www.shadesofgrace. org/2010/05/04/americas-founders-proclamations-for-fasting-and-prayer

Townsend, Matt. "Sifted" (sermon), Harvest Bible Chapel, Philadelphia, Pennsylvania, April 2019 www. harvestphiladelphia.org/media/sermons/month/4-2019/

ABOUT THE AUTHOR

For 18 years, Karen Haag was afflicted with a syndrome called Reflex Sympathetic Dystrophy. In 2012, God miraculously healed her and set her free from physical pain.

Karen enjoys sharing of her journey from pain to purpose. She has always been an avid reader, yet Karen never knew God would lead her to compile her own memoir of pain, suffering, and healing.

As a devout believer in the power of prayer, Karen loves to apply God's Word to her life. She is happiest spending time with family and friends and ministering to others. She enjoys knitting, sewing, and photography.

Karen resides in North Wales, Pennsylvania. She is married to her high school sweetheart, Darryl. They have two married adult children and one granddaughter. The Haags also have a son and grandchild in heaven, who are already living in the eternal presence of God!

Made in the USA
Middletown, DE
03 August 2021